Essentials o. . .....g
Qualitative Research

Qualitative Essentials

Series Editor:
Janice Morse, *University of Utah*

Series Editorial Board: *H. Russell Bernard, Kathy Charmaz, D. Jean Clandinin, Juliet Corbin, Carmen de la Cuesta, John Engel, Sue E. Estroff, Jane Gilgun, Jeffrey C. Johnson, Carl Mitcham, Katja Mruck, Judith Preissle, Jean J. Schensul, Sally Thorne, John van Maanen, Max van Manen*

Qualitative Essentials is a book series providing a comprehensive but succinct overview of topics in qualitative inquiry. These books will fill an important niche in qualitative methods for students—and others new to the qualitative research—who require rapid but complete perspective on specific methods, strategies, and important topics. Written by leaders in qualitative inquiry, alone or in combination, these books will be an excellent resource for instructors and students from all disciplines. Proposals for the series should be sent to the series editor at explore@lcoastpress.com.

Titles in this series:

1. *Naturalistic Observation*, Michael V. Angrosino
2. *Essentials of Qualitative Inquiry*, Maria J. Mayan
3. *Essentials of Field Relationships*, Amy Kaler and Melanie A. Beres
4. *Essentials of Accessible Grounded Theory*, Phyllis Norerager Stern and Caroline Jane Porr
5. *Essentials of Qualitative Interviewing*, Karin Olson
6. *Essentials of Transdisciplinary Research*, Patricia Leavy
8. *Essentials of a Qualitative Doctorate*, Immy Holloway and Lorraine Brown
9. *Focus Group Research*, Martha Ann Carey and Jo-Ellen Asbury
10. *Essentials of Thinking Ethically in Qualitative Research*, Will C. van den Hoonaard and Deborah K. van den Hoonaard
11. *Essentials of Community-based Research*, Vera Caine and Judy Mill
12. *Essentials of Publishing Qualitative Research*, Mitchell Allen
13. *Essentials of Dyadic Interviewing*, David L. Morgan

Essentials of Publishing Qualitative Research

Mitchell Allen

Left Coast Press
Inc.

Walnut Creek, California

Left Coast Press, Inc.
1630 North Main Street, #400
Walnut Creek, CA 94596
www.LCoastPress.com

ISBN 978-1-62958-358-7 hardback
ISBN 978-1-62958-359-4 paperback
ISBN 978-1- 62958-360-0 consumer eBook

Library of Congress Cataloging-in-Publication Data

Allen, Mitchell, 1951–
  Essentials of publishing qualitative research / Mitchell Allen.
    pages cm.—(Qualitative essentials ; 12)
  Includes bibliographical references and index.
  ISBN 978-1-62958-358-7 (hardback)—ISBN 978-1-62958-359-4 (paperback)—ISBN 978-1-62958-360-0 (consumer eBook)
  1. Qualitative research. 2. Authorship—Vocational guidance. I. Title.
  H62.A45685 2015
  808.06′6001—dc23
                          2015029961

Printed in the United States of America

♾™ The paper used in this publication meets the minimum requirements of American National Standard for Information Sciences—Permanence of Paper for Printed Library Materials, ANSI/NISO Z39.48–1992.

Contents

Preface

If the publications section of your CV is 32 pages long and includes half a dozen publications in the top journal in your field, a couple of award-winning university press books, and two pages of "in press" citations, you can send this book back and ask for a refund. This brief volume is for the rest of us, for whom the process of getting published is both as daunting and as challenging as the research you want to publish.

- I would like to use eight photos in the article. Is that too many?
- Can you arrange a book signing for me at the AERA conference?
- Can I hand out my article at the Georgia workshops I give every year?
- Will this be an eBook?

Journal editors field endless questions from junior scholars trying to learn the ropes. How they find time to also read those endless manuscripts is a mystery. Book publishers like me and the acquiring editors we work with at academic presses spend half of our time finding, developing, and producing the books that you see on our website. The other half is spent educating academics on how the publishing business works. These are not idle questions for you; you live in a publish or perish world. Journal editors and publishers like myself are the keys to your success, but most scholars like yourself are not sure how to effectively operate within the publishing ecosystem.

So we regularly sit on panels at the annual meeting of regional and national organizations. One panel is inevitably a set of journal editors advising an audience of grad students how to get their articles accepted. The other panel is always on electronic publishing. Publishers are regularly invited to teach professional development workshops at universities or in conjunction with national organizations.

And we write books on how to get published in hopes of anticipating and answering many of the more common questions. This one is not the first written for academics. The resources section at the end lists a handful of others, some written by very smart people like Beth Luey, Howie Becker, and Bill Germano. This is, though, probably the first guide designed specifically for qualitative researchers.

Why this particular audience for my book? For one, it's an audience I know and have published for a long time. Then there are the differences in this sphere that bedevil qualitative scholars, things your standard survey researcher, econometrician, or forensic archaeologist doesn't have to deal with. More important, my own view of scholarly publishing is that it is a socially constructed, interaction-intensive activity. Who understands that better than qualitative researchers? I circle back to this idea constantly in the book. As a qualitative researcher, you should understand better than most scholars how a system based on social interaction works. You can learn the specifics of how to get published if you use the research tools you already know in the service of advancing your career. Think of getting published as your next ethnography, and the whole process easily falls into place.

It's now time to start your fieldwork.

What's in This Book

Chapter 1 will give you a basic layout of the territory. It will explain that all publishers are not the same, that they are defined by the audiences they try to reach. After a short history of publishing and of qualitative publishing, we'll then describe who the various people inside the publishing house are. Like nationalities where everyone shares the same family name, almost everyone in a publishing house is called an editor. But their job functions are quite different.

Now that you know who you are dealing with, I'll ask you in chapter 2 to widen your viewpoint from the article or book you're trying to write to the entire research project, the various audiences you have for your work, and how you can best reach each of those audiences—academic or not. Then we'll talk about the first major research project for most scholars, your dissertation, and decide what you might want to do with the products of that study.

Chapters 3 and 4 will discuss how to get an article accepted by, and published in, a journal. Unlike what most of those guidebooks and conference panels will tell you, it's not always about how good your research and writing are. My approach is a distinctly social networking one—you're more likely to get published if the journal editor is your friend. And you're more likely to find the right editor to make friends with if you do some ethnographic fieldwork.

Chapter 5 takes these same two themes—networking and research—to the process of getting your book accepted by the publisher of your choice, and about making the right choice. The process is a bit more complicated in book publishing where the target of your networking is not an academic colleague but a publishing professional. But if your research consists of interacting with heroin addicts under a bridge or hospital administrators with white coats and MD degrees, you should be able to talk with an acquiring editor at a publishing house.

Convincing a publisher to take your book almost always involves preparing a book proposal and writing sample for them to review. While each publisher frames it in different language, the information they need is almost always the same. That's what I guide you through in chapter 6, how to prepare a mouthwatering book proposal for a publisher and the decision making process inside the publishing house once they receive it.

Having paved the way for publication with your networking skills, then you actually have to sit down and write the piece. There are several very good guides to writing qualitative research. I've published some of them. People like Laurel Richardson, Harry Wolcott, and Bud Goodall can give you wonderful lessons about writing up a qualitative study. In chapter 7, I distill what I have learned from working with these excellent writers and others. In addition, I offer you what I have learned about how to get started, how to keep going, and how to finish a project. I end with a section on the crucial process of editing your own work.

The day arrives when you finally submit your article or book manuscript to the publisher. Celebrations follow. Wine or martinis are probably involved. Chapters 8 and 9 talk about what happens next—contracts, illustrations, permissions, and other things that accompany an accepted manuscript. I'm not an intellectual property attorney, so don't take the suggestions in chapter 8 as legal advice; find someone who actually knows these laws. Then I'll walk you through the production process, suggesting how you can maximize the chances of your work coming out the way you had envisioned it.

Chapter 10 deals with marketing. No, don't skip that chapter, especially if you think it's the journal's or the publisher's responsibility to advertise your work. There are good reasons to be actively involved in this part of it. I'll explain why and suggest steps you can take to maximize the distribution and readership of your work. Really. Read it. You'll be glad you did.

Chapter 11 is my attempt to give a perspective on at least a few issues related to electronic publishing—eBooks, open access, do-it-yourself web publishing, and some possible scenarios for the immediate and distant future landscape of qualitative publishing in an electronic world. If it sounds a bit fuzzy, it's because predicting the future is not a particularly reliable skill.

If you're still wanting more, there are some useful resources and a bibliography at the end. If you are still looking for excuses to delay finishing your own article, you'll have to resort to Facebook or Instagram. I'll have done what I can to divert you.

So, pull out your notebook or tablet and start taking notes. We're going into the field.

Acknowledgments

When you get to chapter 7, you'll see that I recommend keeping the acknowledgments short: two or three pages at most. That means I have to live within those boundaries myself. Thanks go to...

My publishing mentors: My first publishing boss and uncle, the late Joseph Lawrence. George and Sara Miller McCune, Al Goodyear, Betsy Schmidt, Steve Rutter, and Judy Rothman, all of whom I worked with at Sage Publications. I started as an intern at Sage at age 25, a temporary measure while figuring out my life trajectory, and then worked for them for 25 years.

C. Deborah Laughton, Methodology Publisher at Guilford Press, who developed the publishing workshops with me that resulted in this book. Her fingerprints are all over it, and I probably owe her some of the royalties on it.

I have had endless discussions about publishing with thousands of academics. Many of them have taught me as much about publishing as I taught them. They certainly taught me everything I know about academia, qualitative research, and academic writing. Thanks go to my many qualitative research tutors: Peter and Patti Adler, Russ Bernard, Norman Denzin, Carolyn Ellis, Bud Goodall, Hilary Hughes, John Johnson, Yvonna Lincoln, Maria Mayan, Janice Morse, and Harry Wolcott, among others. I have also learned much through surprisingly unguarded conversations with other publishers, many of whom have ended up friends. On the personal side, many thanks to friends who have made both my publishing and personal lives a joy. Often those two lives were indistinguishable.

Many thanks also go to the organizers of numerous qualitative conferences who allowed me to teach workshops on publishing that resulted in this volume: International Congress of Qualitative Inquiry, International Institute on Qualitative Methodology, ResearchTalk, National Association of Professional Anthropologists, and Israeli Qualitative Research Association. The hundreds of attendees at these workshops taught me much by their enthusiasm and their perceptive questions.

I've been writing on this topic for a while. Pieces of several chapters appeared in other places: part of chapter 3 in the blog of the International Institute for Qualitative Methodology (Allen 2014), sections of chapters 5 and 6 in the *Cultural Anthropology Methods Newsletter* (Allen 1992a, 1992b), part of chapter 9 in the *International Congress for Qualitative Inquiry Newsletter* (Allen 2015).

A multitude of thanks go to those who read drafts of this manuscript and made suggestions; they were always improvements on the original. These brave souls include Stephanie Adams, Arthur Asa Berger, Jess D'Arbonne, C. Deborah Laughton, and Janice Morse. I especially need to acknowledge Tony Adams, who volunteered without coercion or bribery to do the index.

Finally, but certainly not least, thanks go to my family who have put up with my endless travel, cheerfully accepted recruitment for doing tedious jobs for Left Coast, and suffered through regular boring dinner conversations about academics and academic publishing. Thanks, Vida, Josh, Elena, Alexis, Mike, Lily, and Eli, for everything.

Chapter 1

Inside the Black Box

Publishing is a business. Like McDonald's. Bank of America. Google. Standard Oil. The neighborhood Korean-run convenience store. The coke dealer under the railroad bridge. In our late-capitalist world, it's make money or die. The irony here is how publishing houses make money—on your intellectual property. Those warehouses full of books—they're the unsold ones. They're not assets to the company, but liabilities, taking up space, charged inventory storage fees by the distributor, taxed by the government. Useless. Other than that, there's little to own—some ratty office furniture, a bunch of computers, and occasionally a warehouse building on the other side of the tracks.

What *is* valuable to the publisher is all that intellectual property, all those contracts for books and articles that you, the author, signed and returned without a second thought. Maybe you read them first and, because of the frightful legal language, signed, scanned, emailed, and hoped for the best. What you have that a publisher wants is your ideas. Your words. That's what enriches them, the ability to package and sell the intellectual property created by you and thousands of other scholars. Like you once worried about hiding your diary from your parents, you need to protect your intellectual property.

Protecting your intellectual property is all about that request to "sign a contract" for publication of your book, article, or other writing.

With few exceptions, the signed contract transfers the ownership of that material to the publisher. You may have written it, but it's no longer yours. Somewhere in that skyscraper on Fifth Avenue, or the warehouse at the edge of your university town, along with all those jumbled filing cabinets, dusty computers, and office copies of books, sit file drawers of signed contracts, the crown jewels of the publishing house.

The issue in publishing ethics that riles scholars the most is this link between publication and capitalism. Scholarly writing is sold by global media conglomerates at high prices with little benefit going back to the researcher. Scholarly ideas become commodities, assessed for their commercial potential as much as for their intellectual contributions, under a capitalist-controlled publishing model. Unfortunately, global capitalism is likely to be here for a while, probably for our collective lifetimes. Get over it.

You're in this environment and, as scholars, there are few ways out. You need to publish. Your dean tells you that. Your department chair. Your colleagues. And, for all the lip service about the importance of service and teaching, you're still mostly judged and rewarded on your publication record. You have to play this game to be a successful academic.

What I'm going to try to do here is give you a perspective on the rules of the game so you can strategize to be more successful. As qualitative researchers you know that everything is contingent, socially constructed, enmeshed in human desires, goals, and interactions. Don't think for a moment that publishing is any different. The best scholars aren't always rewarded with voluminous publications. The mediocre aren't always penalized by being kept out of the key journals and book publishers. Yes, you should do good work. But also you should know the rules. That will help you succeed.

If there is any consolation here, it is that you are a qualitative researcher. Though the qualitative enterprise ranges from people conducting semi-structured interviews as part of large, well-funded biomedical research projects to conceptual artists translating research into abstract sculptures in public parks, you have at least one thing in common with other qualitative researchers. You're trained to deal with these contingent, socially constructed situations. You should even be good at it. Unlike the engineer or biochemist, human interactions are your specialty. Read on, I'll teach you how to use it.

Dimensions of the Publishing Industry

As qualitative researchers, you will first want to know the nature of the domain you are studying before you get too deeply into your ethnography. So we'll start with some current (2013–2015) statistics, at least about publishing in the United States. Don't worry, you won't have to do any multivariate analyses. Consider this your village survey.

- There are almost 1.5 million books published in the United States every year. Eighty percent are self-published (Bowker 2014).
- There are almost 100,000 academic journals, publishing 1.8 million articles a year (journalseek.net). About 10,000 of them are open access journals (doaj.org).
- The US publishing industry is close to a $30 billion business (Milliot 2014).
- Amazon is the largest customer of almost every book publisher in the United States, maybe the world (Milliot 2015).
- Currently eBooks represent about 20 percent of all book sales, and have flattened off from their phenomenal growth (Milliot 2014). Fiction is the most common category sold as eBooks. It is a much smaller percentage of scholarly books. At Left Coast, my company, it was 5–6 percent of sales in 2014.
- Of the 12 largest publishing companies in the world, four of them are academic journal publishers (Milliot 2014).
- Of the world's 50 largest presses, two of them (Oxford, Cambridge) are university presses (Milliot 2014).
- Publishers need to earn money to stay in business. That's the capitalist way. It applies equally to Fortune 500 publishers and to university presses and small poetry establishments.
- Some of these presses rake in profits that seems outsized to their role as conveyors of scholarly knowledge. Elsevier, for example, reported a 36 percent net profit in 2011 on sales volume of $3.2 billion (*Economist* 2011). Even the not-for-profit Oxford University Presses reported sales of $1 billion in 2010–2011, with a surplus (read "profit") of 19 percent (Oxford University Press 2011, p. 5). Impressive.

- Smaller academic presses don't command anywhere close to this rate of profitability, if any, so scale seems to matter. In the global flow of scholarly information, big is more sustainable than small.

- When it comes to academic publishing, there are more articles out there to be published than there are journal issues to fill and more books waiting to be published than there are publishing slots at all the legitimate scholarly book publishers. It's a buyer's market. You're the seller. You need to sell a journal editor or a publisher on your work.

I'll help you with that last point.

Why should you listen to me? I have experienced almost 40 years in academic publishing—first with two medium-sized scholarly presses (Sage, Rowman & Littlefield), then with two presses (AltaMira, Left Coast) that I started myself.

I've been responsible for publishing almost 1,500 books, started 30 or 40 new journals, and brought many existing journals to the companies I worked for. I served as editor of two journals for a brief period. I've been responsible for publishing books and journals in most social science and humanities fields and the professional fields related to them. I was actively involved in the growth of publishing qualitative methods and qualitative studies, launched half a dozen qualitative journals, and published several hundred qualitative books. And, as a PhD (UCLA) and adjunct university professor (Mills College) myself, I've been on both sides of this process. I have the scars to prove it.

A Short History of Publishing

The tension between publishers and authors of texts goes back to the very beginnings of writing. From ancient Mesopotamian royal and temple archives, to Greco-Roman libraries, to medieval monasteries, those who wrote usually did so beholden to those in power, whether it was the temple, palace, or church. Most authors in medieval and early modern times were sponsored by a patron, who commissioned, protected, encouraged, and usually controlled the nature of their work (Finkelstein and McCleery 2005, p. 72). It was only with the development of mass produced texts afforded by Guttenberg's printing press that the concept of a printer/bookseller was invented as someone who both produced books and marketed them to buyers (Hellinga 2007, p. 217). They became the patron of the author and, as before, controlled his or her work. Some of these booksellers morphed into the earliest publishers in the nineteenth century (Finkelstein and McCleery 2005, p. 86). The actions of early European printers/publishers were often restricted by state regulations and censorship, such as the British Licensing Act of 1662 (Feather 2007b, p. 524). That tension between the publishing industry and the state over control of publications has carried forward to this day. The producers of the contested commodities, the authors, were rarely considered in the conflicts between power and commerce. It was only with the advent of author copyright in the eighteenth century that rights of the author to his or her works finally began to be considered (Finkelstein and McCleery 2005, p. 75–76). But even then, control of publication usually still rested in the hands of the publisher.

As the distribution of publications went from local to regional to national to global, the need for large global systems to advertise availability became crucial to the success of published work. These mechanisms exist within the current commercial publishing infrastructure. Publication of a new book in English anywhere on the globe is routed through the databases of RR Bowker in the United States or Nielsen in the UK to bookstores, academic libraries, and library wholesalers worldwide. Journal articles are similarly publicized through systems such as Thomson-Reuters Web of Science or EBSCO Discovery. These systems connect with search engines to make the availability of these ideas known to scholars everywhere. The lone scholar wishing to reach colleagues in Munich, Mali, Myanmar, and Minnesota could not possibly duplicate this system. The global information flow favors large-scale media institutions.

Even the idea of a publishing "industry" is a misnomer. Publication outlets range from the lone scholar posting her latest data or musings on the web, to university-based publication outlets for faculty and students, to not-for-profit professional publishers, including university presses and other not-for-profit organizations. For-profit presses range from the miniscule one-book publishing operations of enterprising scholars to the publishing arms of global media conglomerates. A similar panoply of publishing establishments produce scholarly journals, newsletters, and other periodicals. More recently, there has been the emergence of a group of digital archives to house raw data and scholarly analyses.

An Equally Short History of Qualitative Publishing

Qualitative research has been around as long as academic publishing. Most social science fields and professions, like education, social work, and nursing, began by writing descriptive pieces about their findings. Case studies ruled.

With the advent of the computer age in the 1950s, social scientists thought they could really do "science" with massive computer runs. In my early years of publishing, I was involved in publishing lots of political scientists producing the results of multi-year, multi-institutional, multi-national projects that were attempting to quantify such easy concepts as the causes of war and peace. Lots of books got produced and, as you all know, war disappeared.

Anthropology, original home of ethnography, was always qualitative. And, as a result, there was little need for anthropologists to be explicit in writing about their methods. It was a craft, hand taught by senior members of the guild. Other than the British *Notes and Queries in Anthropology*, they didn't produce a field methods text until Pertti Pelto's *Anthropological Research* in 1970. Conversely, qualitative sociologists, defensively posturing against their much more numerous quantitative colleagues, wrote much in this area: Blumer, Strauss/Glaser, Becker, and Garfinkel were all pioneers in self-consciously writing about their qualitative strategies. A few university presses published significant numbers of qualitative studies by sociologists and anthropologists back in those early days.

Best known for publishing qualitative research is Sage Publications, which began doing so in the late 1970s. I was privileged to be part of Sage's development, responsible for its qualitative books from 1980 until 1995. A journal entitled *Urban Life And Culture* (now *Journal Of Contemporary Ethnography*) fit their urban studies publishing program and was launched in 1971, product of a group of West Coast symbolic interactions who studied deviance and everyday life on the urban fringe. Accompanying the journal were a series of ethnographies of urban life, John Johnson's Sociological Observations series, and Sage's first qualitative methods book, Jack Douglas's *Investigative Social Research* (1976).

Beginning in the mid-1980s, the success of Sage's quantitative and program evaluation publications led to the nascent world of qualitative researchers, then located mostly in the fields of education and sociology. A parallel series to Sage's little green statistics books, in blue, was begun in 1984. Through its various acquisitions editors working in multiple disciplines on both sides of the Atlantic, Sage began collecting a stable of key writers. Egon Guba, Yvonna Lincoln, Matthew Miles, John Creswell, David Fetterman, and Robert Stake were signed up from education. William Foote Whyte, Norman Denzin, and Anselm Strauss came from sociology. Anthropologists Russ Bernard and Harry Wolcott began publishing texts for Sage. Janice Morse brought in an audience of nursing researchers with her journal, *Qualitative Health Research*. John Van Maanen and others came from management and organizational studies. All wrote key texts for Sage in the late 1980s and early 1990s. The capstone publication became Denzin and Lincoln's 1994 *Handbook Of Qualitative Research*, whose four editions (number five coming in 2016) have tracked the changes in qualitative research ever since. Nor was Sage alone. Academic Press, Routledge, University of Chicago Press, Temple University Press, and others actively expanded their qualitative publishing during this time.

By the mid-1990s, interest in qualitative research had boomed in various scholarly and professional fields—management, public health, psychology, communication, gerontology, family therapy and, eventually, political science. Discipline-focused qualitative books appeared to match the generic ones. Imaginative variations in qualitative methodology, many taken from other research fields, developed: focus groups, action research, discourse analysis, phenomenology. A raft of different publication types offered something for everyone, from textbooks to journals to text analysis software. Publishers working in various academic fields were drawn toward qualitative research because of the growing interest in those fields. Sage's methodology editors moved to other publishing houses—AltaMira Press, Guilford Press, Left Coast—and created competing lists of books. More recent movements toward arts-based research, community-based research, and mixed methods research represent yet another generation of this growth.

Open the Door, Look Inside

So how do publishers monetize the filing cabinet of signed contracts and the jumble of words that you and many others spewed out on your computers? How do they acquire capital, real financial capital, the kind that gives vice presidents leased Mercedes and trips to the Bahamas, not the kind of social capital that exists in the academic world?

Traditionally, it's been a straightforward process. Take your intellectual property, prettify it with some good editing, design, and an attractive cover; proofread it; print it; put boxes of it in a warehouse, then promote it to interested scholars like yourself or to the libraries you haunt. That model has been working since the start of the Gutenberg publishing enterprise.

To accomplish all this most efficiently, large publishing houses are broken into departments or divisions. Even the term for these institutions is worth noting. A publishing "house" rarely looks like a house if it's more than a two person operation (though Left Coast worked out of our suburban home for seven years). "Publisher" is another standard term. Or a "press," though it is extremely rare that you'll find anything more than a photocopy machine resembling a printing press in their offices.

Table 1.1: Divisions of a Publishing House

- ► Acquisitions
- ► Production
- ► Distribution
- ► Sales and Marketing
- ► Administration and Finance

Let's open the front door of a hypothetical publishing "house," Qualitative Press, Inc., and see who is inside.

The book division takes up the first two floors. Turn left at the door and you'll find the acquisitions department, the friendliest and most familiar to scholars. These **acquisitions editors** (also called sponsoring editors) are responsible for finding and selecting the books the press is going to publish. They usually have to answer to (and convince) an **editorial director** or **publisher** that your idea is a good one. Book acquiring editors are also the ones who work with you to get your manuscript finished and ready to produce. In large textbook publishers, they might also be assisted by **developmental editors** who help with the organizing, writing, fact checking. Most scholarly publishing can't afford the luxury of a developmental editor; that work is on you or someone you hire.

When the book manuscript is done and approved by whichever method the publisher chooses, a honeycomb of production workers varnish and polish the MSWord manuscript you turned in. They're all relegated to the basement of this publishing house. A **copyeditor** will look at your use of which/that, it's/its and other things that you forgot from high school English. They'll also make sure your references conform to one of the accepted style guides and, if there's time and money for it, even polish up your language a bit. A **designer** will create a format for those words to appear in and turn it over to a **typesetter** (also called a **compositor**) to pour your words into that template. A **cover designer** will be working on your book cover, a key sales tool. The typeset text will usually be sent to you to review for errors and usually sent to a professional **proofreader** as well. Book indexing happens at the end of the production process, the **indexer** being a different kind of expert. You will probably have little contact with any of these people, only the **project manager**, who is responsible for choreographing all these steps, including your participation, into the semblance of a dance. One day, the project manager will magically announce that the book is "off to the printer." Most publishers do not have their own printing press, but utilize the services of a professional **offset printer**, a small group of whom do short run books, the kinds of books that sell in the hundreds, not thousands. Harry Potter books were not printed by short-run printers. More common today, your publisher will be using a **digital printer,** someone who owns a fleet of glorified copy machines that are able to print one copy or 10,000 at will that are almost indistinguishable from books printed by offset.

While these worker bees are busy with your deathless prose, you'll probably hear more from the marketing and sales departments (second floor, past the lunch room), responsible for getting the word out about your book. Most books in large houses are assigned a **marketing manager**, responsible for your book and the others in your field. We will talk about marketing tasks in chapter 10. Publishers who specialize in textbooks or trade books might also have **sales reps,** a rarity in selling academic books, to call on bookstores or professors. **Customer service reps** handle phone calls and emails from prospective customers or organizations wishing to purchase.

Often these customer service reps are attached to the **distribution** arm of the publisher, where the books are housed and shipped. Most publishers farm out these functions to a distribution company because this is one area of publishing in which economies of scale have a strong financial impact. Other than being the place where you send your friends to order your book, and where you yourself can order discounted copies for your aunt and your academic mentor, you are unlikely to have much contact with this area of the press.

Overseeing all of this work will be an **administrative and financial staff** (take the elevator to the penthouse. You'll need a special badge to get in). These people do what similar departments do in most businesses: coordinate and oversee the operations of the other departments; handle human resources, cash management, and bill paying; make sure there are enough cartridges for the printer and toilet paper for the bathroom; and perform other critical business functions.

The journals division is on the third floor and will be divided similarly to the book division. **Journal acquisitions editors** help identify new journals to start or acquire and work with an academic journal editor.[1] The **journal editor** is usually an academic located at a university and so won't be around when you stop by. The production department is much more like an assembly-line than the book division (see more in chapter 9), and the marketing department spends most of its time talking with their key customers, university libraries, not professors like yourself. The distribution department is much smaller, as few journals are warehoused and mailed these days, and customers primarily consist of a coterie of libraries, not individuals. The journals division will have a good sized tech department, or lease out their technological functions to a third party for their online journal presence. Administrators and financial experts for journals are also located in the penthouse.

The Editor as Ethnographer

We started this chapter by pointing out that you need to find a way to convince people in a publishing house to publish your work, your articles or your book. Now that you've seen the lay of the land, where do you start?

It's pretty evident with the journal. Usually the journal editor, an academic like you, is the gatekeeper. She[2] speaks the same language that you do. No problem here. A good journal editor assumes the viewpoint of a generalist, someone who sees and encourages the wide range of work appearing in the area covered by the journal.

Inside the book publishing house, you want to find the acquisitions editors. They are the ethnographers of academic life. Their job is to know the power structure of your discipline, the kinship chart, the methods of subsistence, who are the Big Men and Big Women, what causes warfare between moieties. What topics are taboo. What people talk about in everyday life. The lived experiences of academics in your field. This is the research they do to decide whom to publish, who should review which manuscripts, who would be valuable for an endorsement quote for the back cover.

They're ethnographers, just like you, except you belong to the tribe they're studying. Want to know what is going on in your field? Ask an experienced acquiring editor. This is good news for qualitative researchers. Most acquiring editors understand what you do; they do the same thing. With that hope, let's start figuring out how to get published.

Chapter 2

Start With Your Research Project

No one engages in qualitative research with the purpose of writing an article. There is a research question, a social setting, a problem of human life that compels you to begin the journey. It is the question that drives you. Articles or books are just the products of that question.

What you have learned is not only of interest to you. Your colleagues also should be interested in your findings, and others in your methodology, theory, or applications to practice. Students may be helped by what you've learned. Policymakers might rethink their ideas based upon your information. Sometimes your findings will be valuable to a community or group you've studied. Some of your work has more general application. Occasionally, the Holy Grail of "The General Public" is invoked, though the public is not general and is rarely universally interested in any single project.

Your Many Audiences

Thus, your work will likely have multiple audiences. When considering what to publish out of your research project, start by thinking through a complete publications plan, not just the one article you hope to write for the prestigious journal you expect will accept it. In this way, a study might have multiple articles emanating from it: one

Essentials of Publishing Qualitative Research by Mitchell Allen.
27–33. © 2016 Left Coast Press, Inc. All rights reserved.

for a methods journal, one for a theory publication, several for different disciplinary journals that touch upon your work, one for the applied journal or newsletter.

Don't stop there. If there is community interest in your work, reflect on how that community accesses information. Offprints of your refereed articles won't do it. They won't be read. Maybe a public presentation, a single page fact sheet, or an informative video is how community members will best understand how your work applies to them. If you're dealing with youth, perhaps a hip hop song or a video game in which your findings are embedded will better explain your message. If there is student applicability, writing a textbook—one which explains your work in terms of a naïve, younger reader—will be more useful than standard academic prose. And the general public? A blog, an op-ed piece for a magazine, or posting on a well-known website might garner a larger audience than using the traditional methods of academic publishing.

These ideas are not mutually exclusive. You can do ALL of them, each publication addressed to a different audience in a format that that audience will best understand.

Similarly, the language you use will vary depending on the product. You can Foucault and van Manen all you want in the article for *Qualitative Research*, but trying to explain the applicability of Foucault in a community meeting is a recipe for disaster. Words like 'unpacking,' 'materiality,' 'panopticon,' or 'discourse' do not regularly get bantered around at the Safeway Market just a few miles from campus. Save the specialized jargon for your colleagues.

Context also matters. While the history of the important research question you are studying might be self-evident to you and everyone in your research community, you shouldn't assume the same of level of understanding from students or the public. In one of my archaeology courses, I tried to explain how the politics of heritage affected the Middle East peace process. What I wasn't expecting was that the group of sophomores in my class had too little context in the history of the Middle East conflict over the past 100 years to understand the importance of the politics of heritage. I had to fill all that in before the subject of my discussion made sense to them.

Begin by identifying each of the potential audiences for your work. Research how to best reach each of these audiences, the language they use, the contextual knowledge they will need in order to understand what you have learned and apply it. How much better and broader your research will be received when you match the medium to the message.

Table 2.1 Your Audiences and Ways to Reach Them

Academic article	Academic colleagues
Professional book	Academic colleagues
Textbook	Students
Popular book	Public interested in your findings
Professional magazine article	Professional colleagues
Op-ed piece	Policy makers and analysts
Glossy brochure	Community groups
Video, YouTube	Community members
Electronic game	Youth, children
Blog	People with too much time on their hands

The fact that you are doing a qualitative study is an advantage for your ability to appeal to many audiences. You tell stories, you create compelling characters, you use the tools of the creative writer (see chapter 7) to present serious research findings. Qualitative studies are advantaged in that they have the capacity of appealing to many audiences. Don't be afraid to use these tools.

Along with this opportunity, qualitative studies also pose many challenges for the researcher. You have all those hundreds of pages of field notes and interviews that have to be condensed into a coherent story. Unlike the quantitative pronouncement that "a 67 percent majority of people feel...," you have to address the ambiguities that those 67 percent won't tell the survey researcher. And you need to define and describe the word "feel" in human terms. You also need to address your own complicity, involvement, and perspective with these amazing humans you studied. There's nothing simple about writing up a study. Ask any qualitative researcher.

There is also the expectation that you know how to write. Can you craft the story to do justice to the thoughts of 86-year-old Maybelle, in whose living room you spent many afternoons? Or Dejean, whom you followed on the streets night after bitter cold night as he did his rounds? How do you capture their lives, views, foibles, and genius in your words? If you can't tell a good, compelling story, can you really be an effective qualitative researcher?

For the moment, let's leave aside the need to justify the rigor and replicability of the qualitative work you do to the non-qualitative scholars in your department. To explain yet again how qualitative studies can be as theoretically robust and rigorous as any pre- or post-testing they do. That bias is a benefit, not a deficit, in your work.

Ambiguities of field work. Ethical challenges. Overwhelming amounts of data. The defensive posture against those who denigrate your research tradition without understanding it. The literary imperative. To be a good qualitative researcher, you've gotta be a good scholar. A really good scholar. How many of your more traditional colleagues could pull this off? And you've already demonstrated you can do this kind of work effectively at least once... in your dissertation.

Your Dissertation

You pour the champagne in the barren classroom late on a Tuesday afternoon in spring and accept the congratulations of the five committee members whose signatures grace your dissertation and who just hazed you through your defense of it. The toughest of them, now on his third glass of Korbel, mutters through the brie and sourdough sandwich in his mouth, "You should get this published."

Well, should you? After all, your committee is urging you to. And your mother would be thrilled to see a book with your name on the cover after all those years of supporting you through grad school. Just think, the congrats at your next professional conference, the review in the *New Yorker*, the publisher book launch party at your favorite bar in town.... OK, stop drifting off into fantasies, this is a serious question.

Should you publish the dissertation?

First of all, the diss will already be made public, hence "published," without your having to do much of anything. Probably, it will be archived through your university and some commercial or academic organization like Proquest. So anyone who really wants to know what you had to say on page 423 can get his or her hands on it. The dissertation is done and soon to be published, even if in fugitive form.

But that's not really what you're asking, is it? If you've read the first half of this chapter, you already know part of the answer. Your dissertation is the first product from this study. Your audience was the five members of your committee. So look again at what I suggest. What are the other audiences for the new knowledge you've created? And how would they best be served by a publication/product of your dissertation? Research articles, YouTube videos, community talks, a book? The answer to that question should get you a long way toward deciding what to do next with this completed research project.

Another consideration has nothing to do with publication decisions and stretches beyond the scope of this book. Your decision should have less to do with all those double spaced pages with standardized margins and more to do with your career strategy. Planning on staying in academia? If so, what are the costs and benefits of getting the dissertation published versus other strategies you might choose to get your career started. If you're going out of the university to another professional career, the same question holds. Is this of any value to me in getting my career off the ground after having been in school since Gloria Steinem was in diapers? So go back to the guy with the brie/sourdough sandwich and talk seriously about your strategy for getting a job to pay off your student loans. The book royalties are unlikely to help much with those loans. If publishing a book will help you—and in fields like history or literature it often will—then go to it. But in most fields that qualitative researchers inhabit, a book is a luxury, not a necessity.

Let's think through your strategy. Your work has had a total audience of five readers so far—those signatures on page 2—and maybe a few friends, relatives, and colleagues you have bullied into reading parts of it. Why not expand the group by sending chapters, reworked as articles, off into the ether? It will get you the feedback of journal editors and journal reviewers (see chapter 3) to get a better sense of what you should do with this as a larger, unified document. Not only will the existence of two or three published articles not hurt you getting a book published down the road, it will help. You can use those articles as a way of building an audience of readers of your ideas. If your intent is to turn these articles into a book, make sure that footnote 1 says "This article is a segment of a larger work on intersectional zombie sexuality that will result in a book publication." And you will have a better sense of the place of your work in the broader field based on the responses of the journal editors and reviewers. A book publisher is also likely to look at your work that way, too—if your ideas are good enough to be published as three articles in three different journals, it's likely pretty good stuff and should be taken seriously.

Those articles are also much shorter and much easier to get out for review and publication than reworking your dissertation as a book. And a cluster of articles will add more lines to your CV than a single book publication will. Build your resume? Give you an understanding of where your ideas fit in the field? Help build an audience? All for a lesser amount of work? Hell, that's surely the way to go.

But wait, the dissertation is already done. It shouldn't require any work at all, other than a last edit. I can just publish it as is, can't I?

Ah, here is the dirty secret about your dissertation. Between the process of finding a publisher for it, the revisions that will almost inevitably be required, and the length of the publication process, it will be several years before you can send mom a copy. That is, if you can get it published at all.

Return to the Big Idea

If your dissertation committee was doing its job, you started the dissertation process with a Big Idea, a broad research question that you sought to answer. The committee carefully and conscientiously had you narrow that focus to a research question you could address in a few years of concentrated research and writing. Similarly, your "I'm gonna interview everyone in Iowa" got narrowed to eight interviews; your dozen methods of triangulated analysis got narrowed to a couple, and the project that would have taken you several lifetimes to complete got focused down to something that could be accomplished in the remaining career trajectories of your aging committee members.

But a publisher wants a book on the Big Idea you started with, not a narrowly constructed study of one small facet of that idea. So all that narrowing will need to be broadened. The literature review of everyone who has worked on this question before, the chapter you were required to condense to 20 pages, will need to be expanded back to a couple of chapters to provide a context for your work. The citation of every theorist who has ever sneezed in the direction of your Big Idea will need to be condensed to only the ones who are relevant. Your mounds of data will need to be further refined and limited to that which most directly addresses your Big Idea. The bibliography will get cut in half. Most appendixes will be excised and the interested reader sent to your archived dissertation. In short, there will typically be a lot of rewriting of the dissertation to turn it from a narrow study that could get completed before your committee members retired to a broad book that a publisher can sell.

While each situation is different, this is usually my advice to junior scholars. Churn out a couple of articles from your dissertation. The raw material is already there, and the work load to convert it into articles is moderate. You will have a better sense of how the outside world views your work, you will have more feedback from a wider range of reviewers, and you will be building an audience for your work. Most importantly, you won't have to dive back into the document to do yet another major revision. At least, not yet.

In the meantime, in addition to your video for community members and blog posts for your friends, you should consider how to get those couple of articles you just churned out published to help launch your career. Turn the page.

Chapter 3

Finding the Right Journal

When your dissertation advisor or department chair asks about your publication plans, she's almost always talking about your articles submitted to and accepted by peer reviewed research journals in your field. After all, the collection of vitae lines you amass that have the volume, issue #, and DOI on them represent the coin of the realm to tenure and promotion committees, granting agencies, and for boasting rights at those late night gatherings for drinks at the hotel lobby bar during the annual conference.

If you ask the average academic how hard it is to get a journal article accepted, the inevitable answer will be, "It's hard, long, time consuming. And, after interminable waits, the answer is usually no or a set of changes to make that might as well mean no." Is Publication Mountain really so unsurmountable?

There Are Lots of Journals Out There

Well, maybe not. After all, there are plenty of options out there. Recent figures highlight the total of 100,000 academic journals (journalseek. net) publishing 1.8 million articles a year (Ware and Mabe 2012). And that doesn't count all the refereed proceedings, edited volumes, annual series, and professional association magazines. How can so much

You have choices.

get published and none of it be yours? It can't. The fact is, you have lots of options.

How do you find the journals that might accept your work? For researchers, the answer is simple... do some research. In qualitative research, while a scattered interdisciplinary area, there are several sources where qual-friendly journals can be found. The Qualitative Report (www.nova.edu/ssss/QR/) hosts a list of over 100 specialized academic journals focused on qualitative articles and links to their web pages. Within your own field, there are undoubtedly journals that are friendly to qualitative work and some that aren't. With a little effort, you can find one—more likely several—journals that will be interested in what you are writing.

What should be of greater concern to the aspiring article writer is another set of statistics. The average scholar reads over 250 articles a year, but spends less than half an hour on each one. Forty percent claim they read the entire article, but there are grave doubts that that figure is accurate (Ware and Mabe 2012). How deeply can you read and absorb a research article in that span of time? So, while it might not be so hard to find one or a few slots in those 1.8 million articles published, it might be harder to get that article read by the people you want to learn from your work.

What does this mean for your publications strategy?

1. Do the research it takes to find the right journal for your article.
2. Make sure people can find your article among the 1.8 million and are intrigued to look further.
3. Write that article in such a way that people want to read page 12 as eagerly as they read page 1.

The rest of this chapter is devoted to the strategy for the first two topics. Look at chapter 7 for suggestions on the third topic.

Table 3.1: A Strategy for Getting an Article Published

- ► Preparing a title and abstract
- ► Creating a list of appropriate journals
- ► Gathering information on the journals on your list
- ► Approaching the journal editor of your first choice
- ► Writing and submitting the article
- ► Waiting… waiting… waiting
- ► Negotiating revisions
- ► Preparing materials to go along with the final manuscript
- ► Celebrating publication!
- ► Marketing your publication

Preparing a Title and Abstract

Standard procedure for writing a journal article: Slave over the research for years. Agonize over every word of the text of the article for months. Eat lots of ice cream whenever you get stuck. Cut 2,500 words out to meet the guidelines of the journal. Finally get the article in the shape you want. Dash off an abstract because the submission guidelines say you need one. Invent a title just as you are about to push the Submit button. Article gone. Then go downtown for another ice cream cone.

Sound familiar?

I'm going to suggest reversing the order. Start with the ice cream cone. Then think about the title and abstract. Seriously think about them before you begin your article. I suggest starting, rather than ending, with a title and abstract for two reasons. First, you're going to find a home for your article before it is completed, and the shape of the article will determine where that home is. Second, when that article gets published, you want people to find and read it. Without a well-crafted, effective title and abstract, that task is made much harder.

So spend time at the beginning finding the right title for your work and crafting an abstract that accurately and comprehensively explains what is in the article. You, like everyone else, use those two items to decide whether this is an article you want to download and read. Search engines use those two items to determine whether your article comes up in a search. The title and abstract are critical for the success of your article. And, if you're going to negotiate a home for your article, you need a good description of what you're doing to begin discussions with journal editors.

Both title and abstract should revolve around the idea of 'keywords.' What terms will signal to readers that your article will be for them? Those terms should end up in your title and abstract. The most important ones should be in the title because that is what readers will see first. If some of those phrases, including their synonyms, don't make it in one place or another, journals will often offer you the possibility of providing additional keywords. The key here is discoverability, maximizing the possibility that potential readers will find your article out of the 1.8 million new ones floating out there.

Titles. The safest way to craft a title is to include as many of those keywords as you can fit in 10 to 15 words (between title and subtitle). "Understanding Zombie Acculturation to California Urban Environments Using Constructivist Grounded Theory" tells the reader a lot about what is in your article, even if it causes them to worry about your grip on reality.

Maybe you want to include something more metaphorical in your title. A good metaphor can attract the reader's attention. No problem, provided the metaphor also connotes the topic. To attach something to the front of our title here, you would do better with "Unlived Experience" using the phrase above as a subtitle than you would if you tried to use "Follow the Yellow Brick Road" or "Of Mice and Men" with that subtitle. A brief quote from one of your interviewees might work as a title with a descriptive subtitle, but only if the phrase you use reflects the key point of the article. In titles, you have a strict budget of words; make each one count.

Abstract. Not much better as budgets go. Published guidelines for most journals will indicate the number of words allowed for the abstract, usually 100–200. Not much space to tell the reader everything important about your article, the kinds of information suggested in Table 3.2. Much of this is straightforward—your population, theory, methods of data collection and analysis. What most abstract writers leave out, though, is the most important thing for the reader—what you found. The tendency is to provide all the processual information and leave it at "if you want to read what I discovered, read the article." Good dramatic setup, but in our search engine-driven existence, it might be too little information to cause the busy reader to download your article. Better to add, "We found that…," and enough information for the reader to know he or she needs to access your piece as support for his or her own work or account for the differences. It's a tough job to fit everything into that short a space, but it also gives you a structure for the rest of the article still to be written. And it forces you to have the article constructed in your head in a way to help you identify the right journal for it.

Table 3.2: What Should Be in an Abstract

- ► Subject, field/subfield/specialty
- ► Scope and purpose of the research
- ► Theoretical models used
- ► Design, methodological strategies, and techniques
- ► Subject population
- ► Key findings and their significance
- ► Any and all keywords that you want this searched on
- ► Make it interesting

Finding the Right Journal

The instructions are right there on the journal website. Second tab on the left. Click a couple of buttons, upload your abstract, your article, input the same user name and password that you have used in fifty other places, type in all that annoying contact information, then wait for the confirmation to show up in your inbox. "Your article has been received; we will respond as soon as the editorial team has a chance to review it."

And then you wait.

And wait.

A month. Sometimes two. Sometimes more. Eventually, the answer comes back in an impersonal email from the editor:

Yes!!... No... Or, most commonly, "Revise and resubmit," along with three sets of obtuse comments that suggest conflicting strategies for you to improve the article before resubmitting it. No wonder the journal *submission* process (note the term used to describe it) is so offensive to most young scholars. Yet you can't avoid the game and succeed in the academy. Nor do you want to; you want your colleagues to read about the research that has you so excited.

How do you find the right journal? That's easy... RESEARCH! If the goal is to find a publication and audience receptive to your particular method, subject, and content, you need to identify which journal those readers read.

What do they read? Probably the same journals you do. So start there. Look at your own list of subscriptions. Which of those journals do you eagerly await in order to scan what they have to offer? How many organizations have you joined in order to get their quarterly flagship publication? Which journals are cited the most in your article? And, of the articles you cite, who do they cite? There are communities of scholars who gather around the same literature. The places where you hang out intellectually are likely to be the places where you will find your own readers. They hang out there, too. Make a list of these and you've finished the first step of your research.

But this is only the first step. The journal you cite often may be highly quantitative, one that you cite because of its content but that you think is hostile to qualitative work. Will they accept qualitative articles? Or maybe there is a timing problem. You need this piece in print quickly because the topic is hot in policy circles, but you've heard sad tales of scholars having their article accepted only to have it wait in the queue for two or three years as the journal works down its backlog. Is that the journal you want to try to publish in? Another publication that sounded very good from the website was filled with typos and grammatical errors when you browsed an article, showing that the editorial team did nothing to ensure professionalism in the articles they accepted. Then there is that journal that publishes interesting stuff but comes out of Zurich and somehow seems to be running three years late.

How do you avoid these publishing disasters when you are looking for a quick-publishing, professionally handled, well-distributed home for your latest creation? That's step 2 in the research process.

Start with the journals' websites. If the last issue listed there is two years old, you have reason to be suspicious that they are not publishing on time. The website should also give you a wealth of other information:

- recent tables of contents will show whether or not the journal has published material in your area, using your theoretical inclinations and your methodology.
- the journal editorial board will often give you a hint of the kinds of articles the journal is seeking. If you recognize none of the names of the board members, maybe this journal is not for you. But if the board is filled with people who populate your citations, you should be encouraged that they will be receptive to your work.
- the website should also contain information about the journal's editor, who in most cases is the ultimate decision maker for journal acceptances. If she comes from a tradition close to your own, you will look at the journal differently than if she works in an area far from your own interests.

From this, you can create a list of two, five, 20 journals that might be receptive to your article.

Table 3.3: Some Major Qualitative Journals

- ► Cultural Studies/ Critical Methodologies
- ► Departures in Critical Qualitative Research
- ► Ethnography
- ► Field Methods
- ► Grounded Theory Review
- ► International Journal of Performance Arts & Digital Media
- ► International Journal of Qualitative Studies in Education
- ► International Review of Qualitative Research
- ► Journal of Contemporary Ethnography
- ► Narrative Inquiry
- ► Oral History Review
- ► Qualitative Family Research
- ► Qualitative Health Research
- ► Qualitative Inquiry
- ► Qualitative Market Research
- ► Qualitative Psychology
- ► Qualitative Research
- ► Qualitative Research in Geography Newsletter
- ► Qualitative Social Work
- ► Qualitative Sociology
- ► Symbolic Interaction
- ► Text and Performance Quarterly

Online, open access journals

- ► Forum Qualitative Sozialforschung (Germany)
- ► Global Qualitative Health Research (USA)
- ► International Journal of Education and the Arts (USA)
- ► International Journal of Qualitative Methods (Canada)
- ► The Qualitative Report (USA)

For more qualitative journals, go to www.nova.edu/ssss/QR/calls.html

(from Carolyn Ellis/Art Bochner's unpublished list and Ron Chenail's The Qualitative Report)

Prioritizing Your Interests

From this list, you need to decide which journal to try first, for the rule in journal publishing is that you can only submit your article to a single journal at a time. When the decision is made by that journal, or when you decide to formally withdraw your submission, then you can submit it to another journal. What might you consider when deciding which journal to send the article to?

- Speed of acceptance and publication
- Size of subscription base
- Available in open access
- Prestige within your discipline
- Aesthetic feel of the publication
- Generalized publication in your field or one focused on specialized subfields
- The general vibes of the journal
- Citation index ranking
- Responsiveness of the editorial team
- Ability to publish color or multimedia elements

Do you need to have a publication in this particular journal on your CV? Do you want to maximize readership? Do you think the article is more appropriate for a specialized or a generalist audience, for your discipline or for an interdisciplinary audience? There is always more than one answer to those questions. Make a list of your priorities, rank them, then look at each journal on how it fits into this scale. When you're done, you'll have a short list of journals that are potential candidates for your publication, including one that ranks at the top of the list.

Citation Indexes: A Discursus

In our neoliberal universities that are becoming ever more focused on counting and accounting, the junior scholar has become prisoner to the citation index. Originally launched as a way to assess the relative importance of journals, it has become a tool used by tenure committees, grant agencies, department chairs, and government to rank the outlets for your ideas. Your list of priorities above might be a long one, but some key decision makers who can affect your career might only be concerned about the citation ranking for the journals you publish in.

Where does this magical number come from? The Web of Science, a private service owned by the Thomson-Reuters corporation, looks at the citations listed in 12,000 journals (which makes it only 12 percent of total number of academic journals around) and counts how many times a journal is cited in the body of these 12,000.[1] The more times a journal is cited, the higher the number. These quantitative figures are then categorized and ranked so that a journal can claim to be "number 12 in the ranking of 93 education journals." Just like TripAdvisor.

Sounds pretty scientific, and the hard science fields have bought into it wholesale. So have university administrators and lots of tenure committees. Wholesale. But a look beneath the final numbers shows some clear biases: the service was started in 1960 and began with a focus on STEM (science, technology, engineering, medicine) journals. So there are a lot of those in the elite 12,000. It was also started at a time when there were far fewer journals in the social sciences and humanities, so it tends to privilege older ones over newer ones. Too bad for new research areas that didn't exist 60 years ago, like qualitative research. Since they count citations from a single journal, fields that are citation heavy—where long strings of citations are the cultural norm—have a distinct advantage. Fields that cite newer material constantly are also advantaged, because the Web of Science only counts citations within the first two years after publication. Forget letting any new idea sink into the discipline and catch on over time if you want a high citation number. Some journals try to game the system by insisting that people who want to publish in their journal cite articles from that journal as a condition of publication. That would bump up the citation number, wouldn't it? In short, newer journals in "softer" fields focused on newer research areas are at a distinct disadvantage. A large percentage of them are not included at all. And many people outside your field, the mechanical engineer and biochemist on your university promotion committee, for example, won't understand why the citation rankings of the journals you publish in are so low, if one exists at all. If you're looking at qualitative research journals, none of which existed in the 1960s, you won't find most of them included.

What is a qualitative researcher to do? Pointing to the biases in the existing system-of-record rarely helps. But because of these inequities, several other citation systems have been created. Each uses a different algorithm, covers a different set of publications, and measures influence in other ways. If the journals you wish to use are not cited in the Web of Science, you might try to convince the committee to let you use one of the others instead.[2] Or buck up and accept the power structure to be insurmountable. In some cases, submitting your article to the journal with the highest citation count is the strategy that best matches your priorities.

Networking Your Article to Publication

If you ask any qualitative researcher if mining basic information from a website provides enough information for a good study, the answer will always come back an immediate "no." You've gotta talk to people, don't you? Network to find a purposive sample. Delve deeply into the lifeworld you're studying, in this case an academic journal.

So, when I suggest that you network your way to publication, it's a strategy that every qualitative researcher will understand instantly. Talk to your friends, your mentors, your colleagues, people on the journal's editorial board, people who have published in the journal. Find out what you can about the journals you have identified from talking to these people.

What should be on your interview schedule?

- Which journals do you publish your work on zombie sexuality in? What has been your experience with them (the journal, not the zombies)?
- Tell me about your interactions with the editor? Fair, open minded, interested in helping junior scholars?
- How long did the review process take? Were the reviewers fair, the reviews substantive? Did the editor guide you to the important parts of the reviews to help you shape revisions?
- Was the journal staff communicative and responsive to questions you had?
- Does the journal have a long queue of manuscripts awaiting production?
- Was the production process smooth and transparent?
- Do you have contact information on the editor? Do you know the editor? Can you introduce me?

The information on the website will undoubtedly raise other questions that you want answered.

Why so many interview questions about the journal editor? It stems from a single insight: the decision to accept or reject an article is usually made by a person, a human, a single individual. A journal editor. One journal editor I know sings with her civic choir. Another is fanatical about Rottweilers. Pants go on one leg at a time. Good days, bad days. In short, they're human. Same as you.

With this understanding, you, the qualitative researcher, are suddenly put in a position of strength. Who knows better how to elicit what someone is thinking (about your article, in this case) than a good qualitative researcher? All those networking, interaction, and sociability skills you learned in grad school and honed in the field can now be brought to play to advance your career.

The journal editor is almost always the final decision maker on which articles to publish. I have this on good authority, having launched several dozen journals for three publishers. The editor is where the buck stops. Those peer reviews? Usually just advisory. Why

Make the journal editor your collaborator.

not make the journal submission gauntlet process interactive, collaborative, and mutually educative? In short, qualitative.

With your carefully constructed title and abstract in hand, it is time to start the conversation with the journal editor. How? At a professional conference, via an email inquiry, or simply pick up the phone. If that's too intimidating, use an intermediary: ask a member of the editorial board whom you know, a colleague in the editor's department, or one of your mentors to introduce you.

"What would be your reaction to submission of an article based on this title and abstract? What would make the idea more attractive to your journal's readers?" It's a semi-structured ethnographic interview you're conducting. Ask her to help you shape the piece so it best fits her vision of her journal. Turn the editor into your collaborator, not your judge. In partnership with the editor, you're more likely to craft a piece that will be looked upon favorably and be accepted for publication.

The conversation with the journal editor will also elicit other information you need on the journal's review process, queue for publication, production processes, and distribution channels. But make sure you read up about these issues at the journal's website before you ask all these questions. Much of the elementary stuff will be posted there.

Part of your task here is to explain your specialty to the journal editor, who has to evaluate articles from every corner of the domain in which the journal publishes but is unlikely to be a specialist in your specific area. She might not know the importance of your work in the literature you are contributing to. The late Bud Goodall (2008, p. 174), author of two influential books on qualitative writing, describes the challenge:

> Don't ever assume they [journal editors] will understand what you mean; it's *your responsibility* to tell it to them in clear, straightforward, non-jargon laden language.
>
> And never, not once *ever*, believe that they will automatically connect your narratives to ongoing theoretical or methodological discussions, or that they will see—without being clearly documented—that your work contributes significantly to the literature in your field and to the marketplace of ideas.

Interaction with the decisionmaker gives you another advantage. If you know who is likely to give you a good review, and who is likely to give you a bad one, you can educate the journal editor on that and explain why. Suggest appropriate reviewers to the editor (include email addresses). She might not choose to use them, but it is better to give her the tools to help the review process than leave the process in the hands of anonymous people and hope for the best. Suggesting your mother, your best friend, or your dissertation advisor is probably not appropriate, but you should be able to identify people who would give you fair but positive reviews.

Pretty Machiavellian of you, isn't it? Getting the journal editor to tell you exactly how to write an article to get it accepted? Not so fast. A relationship usually involves mutual assistance. You're much more likely to get help if you've already provided services to the overburdened journal editor. Send her your resume and ask to review articles for the journal. When the inevitable article comes, do a thorough, helpful review. Repost Tables of Contents on your own social media pages when each issue comes out. And practice simple acts of kindness. If you read an article in the publication that has an impact on you and your work, send a brief note to the editor telling her so. Journal editors get lots of complaints, but rarely get fan letters.

Write the Article

You still need to write a good article, but your buddy the editor is more likely to give you useful answers to questions you may have as you develop the piece. If you get contradictory peer reviews back, she is more likely to give you guidance on which of the comments are important for revising the piece. And, when it's time for a final decision, she's more likely to send the email that says "Yes!!"

Wait, we're at the last paragraph of this chapter and only *now* do you write the article? Yep, that's right—negotiate where you are going to send it before you actually write it. Well, that's a bit unrealistic; you undoubtedly have a rough draft on your computer already, don't you? But with the guidance of the journal editor, you can finish and polish it in such a way that will make it more attractive to the journal. Read on if you want some help on writing it and negotiating the review process that follows.

Chapter 4

Writing, Reviewing, and Revising Your Article

There's a plan in place. You've done enough research to know which journal you wish to send your article to and have several backups if that one doesn't accept it. You've labored over the abstract so that you have a good idea of how it will play out. You've talked with the journal editor and have a good idea what she wants from the piece. Now it's time to sit down and get it done, accepted, and published.

Writing

There is a standard format for the traditional scientific research article that stretches across most fields. This is so engrained in graduate education that I won't elaborate on it here. But if you've never heard of the sequence, Introduction, Methods, Results, Discussion, or IMRAD (www.icmje.org/recommendations/browse/manuscript-preparation/preparing-for-submission.html), then you probably need to find a new mentor or doctoral advisor. By following the template that most researchers use most of the time, you are probably taking a safer route toward getting published.

We know, though, that qualitative research and writing is somewhat different than the standard scientific model. And here is where

---

authors of qualitative articles struggle. Those struggles appear typically in several areas.

Alternatives to the standard model. Your doctoral advisor or your English-major friend is suggesting you be more literary in writing up your study. After all, you've seen Carolyn Ellis and Ron Pelias produce non-linear pieces that truly shine. How far from the standard science model can you stray? It depends on the project. It depends on the journal. Some more applied, more positivist journals will accept qualitative work, but only if it follows the standard article format. Others will give you leeway to develop the piece as you wish. Your interview with the journal editor will clarify the expectations of her journal for you in advance. Skimming the last several years of articles will do the same. If you want to zig but the journal only accepts zags, try a different journal or limit your creative impulses for this piece.

Ultimately, this is your career, your body of work. If you want to experiment with alternate forms, you should do so. With all those journals out there, a little research will tell you where your work might find a sympathetic home. But know that working on the margins does marginalize you and limits your publication options. You need to decide what being different is worth.

Length. This is a perennial problem for qualitative researchers: all those words. The journal word limit is 6,000, but you have 2,000 words of transcripts alone that you want to include. You want to describe the rich social setting in which they were gathered. Your findings are important for policy makers and represent significant improvements to method and theory. How are you going to fit it all in?

The journal's instructions will usually indicate the maximum length of an article. If you really need more space, find out from the journal editor how rigid their guidelines are. In most cases, they are firm except for the most exceptional articles. Journals are given a budget of pages each year, which they cannot exceed. If your article is twice as long as the limit, that means someone else doesn't get published. And you'll be judged twice as severely because of the amount of space you are asking for. Sometimes there are options of separate print and online versions, where the latter is allowed to be longer. Maybe you just need to send it to a different journal that will allow you more leeway. Or shorten it. If you've structured your research program to include multiple publications from the project to multiple audiences, it should be possible to steer some of the material away from this piece and into another one you have on the drawing board.

Coauthorship. You and a friend decide over coffee at University Caffeine how much fun it will be to write something together. After all, you're both studying the lived experience of tuberculosis. But you are doing a mixed method study of a poor urban population and your friend an arts-based piece on the shape of a TB molecule. Things don't go well. You churn out 30 pages of texts and references, your friend a single drawing. Each of you claims your piece required six full weeks of work. Who gets first billing for this piece? Not an uncommon problem. In cases where coauthors ask me to adjudicate order of authorship, I am told by each that he or she did 65 percent of the work. The only way to solve this is to have the division of labor established at the beginning and the order of authorship established before you start. That may be done by the anticipation of who will do the most work, in alphabetical order, or by who needs a publication more for his or her next promotion. Saving this decision until the end can result in catastrophe or lost friendships.

You had better take a close look at your friend before you start. If she never turns in anything on time, you can be sure that this behavior will carry over to a writing partnership.

A more complex form of coauthorship exists in large scale projects where many people are involved in running a laboratory or institute, collecting and analyzing data, and writing up the findings. This occurs often in health research, for example. Who has final say on the article's contents? Who gets credit for the article on which you wrote every word? You are included, of course. But what about those who did the data collection, the coding, those who provided the funding, leadership, and ideas for the overall project? Janice Morse suggests that the order of authorship depends more on the conceptual contributions to the work than on the individual who wrote the piece (Morse 2009, p. 3). This too should be worked out with your colleagues before you sit down and write those 30 pages.

Confidentiality and ethics. Don't you wish you could just be a statistician some times and not have to worry about this? When you turn humans into numbers, the people you have studied are faceless, rounded into a 5 or an 8. But that's not qualitative research. You have interviewed only a few people, and the richness of their lives makes keeping their identities secret difficult, often impossible. Anthropologists, the original qualitative researchers, rarely worried about this in the old days. But then they started studying our own culture. People who could read what they wrote about them. Add the internet and no ethnographic study is immune from community knowledge and feedback. That has its consequences, just ask William Foote Whyte about the reaction from the street corner society (Adler, Adler, and Johnson 1992) or Carolyn Ellis (1995) about blowback from the fisher folk. So how do you keep your subjects confidential while expressing enough of their stories to make them come alive? Morse and Coulehan's (2015) suggestions include using group data instead of individual, pseudonyms, hiding as many descriptive identifiers as possible, obtaining written consent if the details can't be hidden, placing mosaic patches over faces in photos. Other researchers go back to the subjects of their study and offer it to them to read before submitting for publication. Still others choose to collaborate with their subjects so the subjects' perspectives on the topic are heard directly. This still doesn't solve the problem of autoethnography—you probably don't have more than one or two sisters, and they'll know whom you're talking about. If anyone had easy answers about qualitative ethics and confidentiality, there wouldn't be so much written about it.[1]

Blinding. This is the academic version of the confidentiality question. If you are deeply embedded in your work, how do you blind it for reviewers in double blind review setups? Blinding is the process of hiding the identity of the author or the reviewer during the journal review process. In open reviews, the identity of the reviewer and author are known to each other. In single blind reviews, the reviewer knows who the author is but not the reverse. Double blind reviews are supposedly more legitimate because neither reviewer or author is influenced by the identity of the other. The qualitative field runs the full gamut from open (*Qualitative Inquiry*) to double blind (*Qualitative Health Research*). There are advantages and disadvantages to each, as its proponents will tell you. No matter, each journal will have its policy, and you will be expected to follow it. But what if you, like many qualitative researchers, are splashed all over your pages and need to blind your work? Beyond the obvious ideas of removing your name, affiliation, and grant # from the piece, Morse's (2014) suggestions for *Qualitative Health Research* include writing in the third person, replacing self citations with a third person author and date, and citing only your published work, not things in press or conference presentations. The journal's position on blinding could be one of your criteria for deciding which journal to submit your article to.

While these issues are important ones for qualitative researchers who are submitting their articles to refereed journals, there are certainly many other issues in writing qualitative research. I'll talk more about these in chapter 7 and provide a number of other sources for you to consult in appendix A.

The Journal Review Process

You finally pushed the button and sent off that article to the journal, knowing a sympathetic editor would be lovingly receiving it after the numerous conversations you've had about the piece. If it is a solidly managed journal, or if the journal uses one of the manuscript flow software programs, you will receive an acknowledgment of receipt of the article and maybe some vague time frame for its review. If it's not an automated process, you should ask for a confirmation and approximate schedule for decision making.

And then… you wait. And wait. And wait some more. Did we already talk about waiting when we discussed the journal decision-making process? No worries, we can discuss it again. We have a lot of waiting time.

You dutifully teach your classes. Listen to the litany of student psychological problems, sexual issues, financial stresses, and, occasionally, field a perceptive question during your office hours. Spend endless time on meetings with the facilities committee. Try the new Italian restaurant downtown. Collect information on the next grant you're aiming for. Outline the next article in the queue.

And wait. How long can this possibly take?

How long should you wait? You should know the answer to this question if your interview of the journal editor was properly conducted. Or if the journal gave you a time frame in their acknowledgment to your article submission. The simple answer is, "Too long." The more complete answer is that the schedule is generally no longer in the hands of the journal editor.

In defense of journal editors everywhere, they too are spending a lot of time waiting. Waiting to get through the queue of submissions to look at each piece. Waiting for time between their other professional commitments to research appropriate reviewers. Waiting for reviewers to respond to their email and agree to review your article. And then waiting on those reviews. Usually three reviews, sometimes more, sometimes less. The process moves as quickly as the slowest reviewer. Most journal editors will give their reviewers a time frame in which they want a response. Most reviewers will do it when they can, or when they want to. If your reviewer has been called away by a sick mother or two weeks of fieldwork in South Africa, you won't know that. Generally, the journal editor won't either. So cut her some slack.

And so we all wait. Good journal editors will pull the plug on a recalcitrant reviewer after a certain number of weeks and send your article to a backup person. Or do with fewer reviews. But all this takes time.

How long should you wait? As long as they told you to in their initial contact. Then feel free to gently remind them of the schedule they promised. It might prompt a reminder to the reviewers from the journal editorial office. If nothing happens, ask again in two weeks. Gentle, sympathetic (remember, they're hostage to the reviewers, too) pressure is likely to get the most expeditious results.

And shit happens. A reviewer blows off the assignment. The journal editor gets refused by half a dozen reviewers she asked. The journal is coping with a huge influx of manuscripts that all arrived with yours during the week that summer vacation ends. The semester ends and the editorial assistant goes to Tahiti for the holidays leaving no one with the new password for the review database. The editor had pneumonia. But most times, your subtle pressure gets you the kind of activity that will result in an answer.

What Kind of Answer Will You Get?

The journal review process, when it works, is truly a wondrous system. Some smart, hard-working strangers are volunteering to read and critique your work so that it is better than what you were able to construct alone. For all the complaints about the system, a set of good reviews is golden to a junior scholar. Receiving the differing perspectives on your ideas from incisive readers should resonate to the qualitative researcher, no matter how hard it is to swallow what often seems to be unwarranted criticism. It may be difficult to sit and wait for people to tear your work apart, but if the goal of the critique is to provide you with advice on making your work better, it is worth the wait.

Finally, after that endless amount of time, the terse email arrives.

- "NO. We don't believe the article is appropriate for our journal. Here are the reviews."
- "YES. We are accepting your article. It is scheduled for the fall issue."
- "YES. We will publish your article with a few minor emendations, as follow… Please address these points and send the article back in."
- "REVISE AND RESUBMIT. Your article undoubtedly has merit but is not yet ready for publication. Here are the reviews. Please make these changes and resubmit."

Let's take each response separately.

No! ☹

If the answer is no, go to the next journal on your list created from your research of appropriate journals. Life is too short to mourn over a no answer, and you have 100,000 journal options. Most journals have a rejection rate of over 50 percent, some well over 90 percent, so you're not alone. Rejection is part of this process. As we have discussed, there is more than one appropriate journal for any article. This journal has done you the service of providing you with feedback on your article. Pick what you think useful from the reviews and incorporate it before sending the article on to the next publication. Then take one further step: Thank the journal editor for her consideration and, if possible, ask the editor for an explanation of what led to the negative decision. Don't think that this will cause her to change her mind, but it should give you more insight on what you need to do to revise the article. It also leaves the door open for the next article you wish submit to this journal and gives you a better idea of what the journal editor is looking for.

Before sending it to journal 2, remember to review the guidelines for that journal and your notes from discussions with the editor. You may have to tinker with the article a bit to fit the second journal editor's requirements.

But what if journal 2 and journal 3 (and 4, 5, 6) also reject your piece? If no one wants it after multiple tries, then it's time to rethink what you've presented and how. You should have lots of feedback between the reviewers' comments and your dialogues with the journal editors. Put it aside, let it sit. At worst, you may have to drop the piece. You will write more than one article in your career, so this is not a life threatening decision. But some distance from the piece might allow you to reimagine it in a fashion that will make it more palatable the next time you try to publish it.

Yes! ☺

If the answer is yes, pull out that special bottle of cabernet and exult at your good fortune. Congratulations, you'll have at least one of the 1.8 million articles this year. But stop after that first celebratory glass. Well, if it's a top-notch journal, have a second glass. Getting the acceptance, with or without revisions, is not the time to rest on your laurels. It's time to get the accepted article into print.

If you've been asked to make revisions, please do so. Quickly. Most journals have a queue, and your place in line is determined when they have your final manuscript in their hands, not when the acceptance letter goes out. If there is any concern about the revisions you still need to make, see the next section.

Revise and Resubmit

With trepidation, you open the email from the journal editor. It's the dreaded "revise and resubmit." And three reviews, each in a different funky font. Just like the Three Bears, Reviewer 1 says it needs more theory; Reviewer 2 thinks it had too much. Reviewer 3 describes the critical realist article that she would have written if she had your data to work with. But that's her article, not yours. The journal editor's instructions are to make the changes and resubmit the article, preferably within 30 days. WTF do you do now?

Start by having a glass of that good cabernet. Yell at the wall, at your dog, at your BFF about how stupid and inane reviewers are and how the entire peer review system should be damned to hell, and why you should have stayed tending bar where you can collect good tips and go home after your shift and not have to think about it till the next day. You won't be the first person to do this.

Yeah, get it out of your system.

Then, return to your article. If the journal editor is good, her comments will be far more extensive than "make the revisions." She will give you guidance on what is important in the reviewers' suggestions and what can be safely ignored. Those journal editors will all go to heaven and sit at the foot of Saint Citation when their time comes.

More common is minimal guidance from the journal editor. So you need to create your own. Read the reviews carefully, note their inconsistencies and contradictions. Note what is useful for your paper, both little things and big issues. Take the reviews seriously, someone took the time to read your piece and, in the best of worlds, is making suggestions to help make it better.

Then decide whether the suggestions are ones you can make, ones that meet your vision of the paper. If the work suggested requires you to throw away what you've done and start anew, it's probably not worth trying to rework your paper. Write to the journal editor and withdraw it from submission. Politely. And give a brief description of why you are taking that action. After all, you don't know if you'll want to submit something else to this journal in the future.

But if enough of the revisions are doable, if the reviewers' comments will result in a better paper than your original submission, come up with a revision plan. A written one. What points of reviewer 1 will you incorporate and how do you plan to do it? Ditto reviewers 2 and 3. Highlight the inconsistencies between the reviews. Point out the ones that don't seem germane to your vision of your paper; explain why you feel you should ignore those specific comments. And send your plan to the journal editor along with your thanks for the careful, useful reviews.

"Hey, editor, here is my revision plan. This is what I plan to do and why. This is what I plan to ignore and why. Does this plan sound okay to you?" At a minimum, the journal editor will have to reread your paper and the reviews to write you a response. She might have a better feeling about it on second reading. She might give you the benefit of her own suggestions while assessing the reviewers' comments to you. But you already have a relationship with the journal editor, so it shouldn't be difficult to have a discussion on this issue. Negotiate your revisions with her so that you're both clear on what is expected, get her to bless your revision plan.

Then make your revisions. You now have a clear idea of what is expected in your revised manuscript. Having blessed your revision plan, the journal editor will have a harder time saying no if you resubmit the article with those changes made. When you submit the revised paper, include the reviews and the revision plan you and the editor agreed upon. She will probably send the article back to one or more of the reviewers, so ask her to send your revision plan along with it so the reviewers know what you've revised and why (and that she has blessed your revision plan). If you have followed through with your part of the agreed-upon plan, there is a greater likelihood of an acceptance letter coming back from the journal. After all, she told you what you needed to do to create an acceptable article, and you did just that.

It's a social process. Use those skills you've developed as a qualitative researcher to help build your publications record. Then you can break open that bottle of cabernet and celebrate the acceptance of another article. Welcome to the 1.8 million!

Chapter 5

Finding the Right Book Publisher

- *Their sales rep came by just as I finished the manuscript.*
- *I got stuck in a broken elevator with the editor at a conference.*
- *They asked me.*

We hear stories about the author who published with Plagiarist Press or Mediocre Monographs for many different reasons, often with regret. Here I hope to give you a more systematic way of finding the publisher who might be right for your book.

First, don't underestimate the amount of work a book entails. If you know how much work it is to write eight or ten articles, think of finishing a book as being like that, only harder. For once you've written those articles, you now have to create a flow between them so that the reader gets a seamless narrative. Not easy. Furthermore, you need to assess how important a book is to your career. If you're a junior scholar in a field where articles are currency, you may want to hold off writing "the book." You might assess the amount of time it will take you to write it. Beyond grocery shopping and laundry, what won't get done when you're spending every weekend in front of a computer? It will take over your life, just as the dissertation (also a book) once did. It's not a surprise that only a small fraction of first draft book manuscripts submitted to us arrive by the deadline, a deadline usually set by the author.

Three Kinds of Book Publishers

As we discovered in chapter 1, the academic book publishing industry is no longer simple to describe. But let us establish a few of its parameters to boundary our discussion of how to get your academic book published. Traditionally, the industry, like Gaul, was divided into three parts: trade books, textbooks, and specialty books.

Trade books are the ones you found in your local bookstore, when there were still bookstores. They were published by one of the titans of New York—Simon & Schuster, Random House Penguin, HarperCollins—or by a host of smaller titan wannabes. They were distinguished by the fact that the customer was never connected to the publisher because the books were purchased in retail bookstores,

Table 5.1: Differences between Three Kinds of Publishers

Types of Book Publishers	End customer	Marketing target	Marketing strategy
Trade	General public	Bookstore buyer	Sales reps
		General public	Advertising Store display Author tours
Text	Students	Professors	Sales reps Direct mail Web marketing Conferences Free copies
Academic/ Professional	Scholars Professionals	Scholars Professionals Libraries Organizations	Direct mail Conferences Libr. Wholesalers Websites Social Media

a third party. That is still true today, though more and more the third party is Amazon.com, and they have lots of information about you, their customer. The implications of this were many. Advertising went in two directions: from the publisher to the bookstore to convince the bookstore to carry the book, hopefully in large enough volume to display it in the front of the store to get readers' attention, and from the publisher to the customer through mass media (newspaper and magazine ads, billboards, TV ads, talk shows, and so forth) to encourage the book buyer to purchase it "at your local bookstore." Trade books were priced low, discounts given to the bookstore were high (usually the starting point was 40 percent of list price), and the lifespan of the book lasted until the next season's series of books was announced. Then all those unsold books were remaindered—sold to a third party for a small fraction of their original price—to be marketed to consumers at a much lower price at discount bookstores or at the discount tables at the same store that sold them for full price a few weeks earlier.

Discount schedule	Print run	Prices	Shelf life
40% and up	5,000+	cloth $25 +/- paper $8–15	6–12 months
20%	3,000–50,000	Core $50–175 Supplemental $25–50	2–3 years
0–20%	100–5,000	What the market will bear	2–10 years

With the growth of superstores of book chains like Barnes & Noble and Borders in the 1990s, the industry began to consolidate to fewer, larger sales outlets; the fight over discounts between publisher and bookstore intensified as the stores pushed the publishers for volume discounts so they could offer higher discounts to customers. As Amazon.com gradually grew into the behemoth it is today, that trend accelerated. EBooks arrived on the scene at prices less than your chai latte from Starbucks.[1] And, with most people buying books from a single all-inclusive source, the number of publishers grew from 85,000 in 2003 (Poynter 2015) to over 450,000 in 2013 (Bowker 2014). Was the industry growing? No, the five-fold increase in publishers simply represented a huge wave of individuals self-publishing their books and hoping for the Stephen King effect to bring them fame, fortune, and literary acclaim.

Because of the high discounts, short shelf life, and need for mass markets, very few academic writers ever succeeded in this world, though there were (and are) always exceptions, from Margaret Mead and Ashley Montagu to Lilian Rubin and Michael Kimmel. Scholars writing in this genre usually had to make accommodations for the knowledge level of mass readership: minimizing or eliminating footnotes, simplifying arguments and theory, focusing on a story line rather than in-depth analysis. Some scholars did—and still do—this quite well and successfully. But there are very few of them.

Textbooks run in entirely different circles. For our purposes here, we can safely ignore textbooks designed for the elementary and secondary (K-12) classroom, though plenty of scholars in the field of education have written histories of the United States or eighth grade grammars and readings. For college classes, there is again a difference between the publisher's customer and the end purchaser. Remember Jason, the annoying college rep for Megatext Publishing, who comes by once a quarter with doorstop-sized introductory texts by Archibald Effete in hopes you'll order one of them for your freshman class of 600? You're Megatext's customer: if you're sold on their book, Megatext gets 600 sales next semester. With textbook prices shooting up to the $150–200 range, that's big dollars. Textbook publishers can afford to pay for Jason's road trips at Motel 6 and Denny's, his bar bill at the student watering hole, his company car, and a nice bonus in December. They can also afford to hire an assistant professor to pull together Powerpoint lectures, exam items, and a comprehensive website to accompany the text you assign. Because of the enormous investment, most textbooks for introductory classes are developed by Megatext and a few other large textbook publishers. It might cost $1 million to launch a new one. For smaller and more advanced college courses, with a much wider range of acceptable books that serve as textbooks, the major textbook houses have offered some books, but so have independent presses, university presses, and even some trade publishers.

Just like the trade book industry, the textbook world has been transformed over the past decade. For all the complaints about students' lack of performance on their Economics 1 exams, they figured out quickly that they could sell back their (often unread) textbook to the college bookstore in December for some of what they invested in it in August. The bookstores would then resell these books to used book distributors, who would sell the used copies to next semester's crop of students. Used books are considered a better investment for the financially strapped student, even if they have pink marker underlining half the lines on each page. The information flow of the internet helped students find these used books from many sources, so that the publisher's sales of their new textbook in year two were a small fraction of those of year one. Sales of new, unmarked books had all been replaced by used copies, for which the publisher receives no income and the author receives no royalties.

Consolidation has also taken place in the college bookstore industry, so that a majority of them are now managed by the Barnes & Noble or Follett's chains. This means that used textbooks can stay within a single company, shifting from one branch store to another.[2] Alternative supply chains, such as Chegg, Amazon, and direct sales between students have maximized efficiency of the used book marketplace. Hence, textbook publishers produce a new edition of each textbook every five, then three, now two years, to wipe away the used copies of the previous edition floating around, at least until the pool of used copies of the latest edition builds up again.

Large textbook publishers have countered this used book economy through a variety of means: higher prices on new books, so that the first student purchaser subsidizes future used-copy purchases; offering ancillary materials to the instructor such as test banks, canned lectures, websites, pools of illustration, and class assignments;

combining elements from various books to create textbooks tailored to each instructor for each class, which minimizes the possibility of used copies of the same textbook being sold.

Many scholars are engaged in textbook writing; some have made careers (and fortunes) at writing successful introductory books. Many others have written less elaborate textbooks for upper level and graduate classes. Even more have written scholarly works and had them used by their colleagues in classes.

The third kind of publisher is a catch-all, the specialty publisher. Religion books, auto manuals, and test-prep guides all fall under this rubric, as do, of course, **scholarly books.** Here is where scholars present the findings of major research projects, important theoretical advances in the field, methodological treatises to help the research process, and extended think pieces about important themes. These books are sold to college libraries, to authors' colleagues, and to graduate students who will become their colleagues. Unlike the other kinds of books, these are generally sold directly from the publisher to the scholar/student/library. Prices can be high because the markets are small and print runs in the hundreds instead of thousands.

The differences between these different kinds of publishers shows up in many facets of publication—end customer, distribution channel, distribution mechanisms, print runs, discount schedules, royalties, editorial assistance, and others (see Table 5.1).

What Kinds of Books Are You Likely to Write

We will focus on the kinds of books you are likely to write as a qualitative scholar. Most of these fall under the "specialty/academic" category described above.

Scholarly Studies (Monographs). This is the bread and butter of most scholars, but generally not of publishers. A specialized book from your research study will attract your peers and their advanced students, but that's usually a small number of people. Once upon a time, university libraries felt that it was crucial to acquire a complete collection of research volumes, but there are few libraries that still collect that extensively. More and more, academic publishers, even university presses, turn these projects down because of the minimal sales. There are some specialized monograph publishers who will publish lots of these books, but at a cost. The author will often be asked to forego royalties on some or all of the sales and/or pay the costs of editing and typesetting. Marketing will generally be done in clusters: all the publisher's books on medical anthropology are thrust into a single large catalog with little push for any individual title. Prices established on these kinds of works will often be prohibitively high because of the limited sales volume.

This is one area in which the electronic revolution has the potential to ameliorate the problem. Self-published scholarly works occur more and more commonly, often accompanied by databases of original source data, field notes, and other bits of the study. Unfortunately, marketing these works is a skill rarely taught in grad school. You might inform your close associates about your work, but the book is unlikely to get broad distribution. We'll talk about marketing your work in chapter 10. And there will always be questions of legitimacy if the publisher is also the author.

Core Textbooks. Someone is writing all those textbooks that students have to read in your class. It could be you. Don't know how to start one? That's the easy part. Every course syllabus is the outline of a textbook for that class. If the way you approach your subject fits the way your colleagues organize their classes on the same topic—and it probably does fit at least some of them—then you have the makings of a core textbook. "Core" because it is expected to be the main written source of information for students in that class. "Textbooks" because they are assigned by the instructor to be purchased by the student for use in the class. Sometimes they're even read by the students. Textbook titles usually reflect the name of the course, and the content follows the outline of standard material taught in that course.

Textbooks come in all shapes and sizes. Writing introductory texts for large publishers might include being assigned a project manager, developmental editor, photo researcher, and ancillary materials creator. The specific niche within this course will be identified, and you will be asked to write to meet the needs of this niche. A battery of colleagues who teach this course will serve as reviewers and will help direct your work. "Direct" is the correct verb. Your textbook will be field tested and market researched to fit a specific market position. You will not have much leeway in what you write or how you write it

What kind of books will you be writing?

if it varies from the publisher's research on fitting your niche. Most textbooks run 14 to 16 chapters, one for every week in a hypothetical semester. These books have pedagogical features (such as exercises and online resources) to help the student master the material.

Not every core textbook is this elaborate. Smaller publishers, or smaller books from big publishers, might look much more traditional—publisher and author agree on the level, style, and structure of the book, author delivers a manuscript, reviewers (also instructors of that course) give feedback, author revises. Publisher publishes. Sometimes everyone makes money on this. Another variant is the *brief text*, where just the basics of the course are presented in highly abbreviated form. This allows instructors to offer the basic information while pairing the brief text with other readings of their choice. *Text-readers* are another variant: the basics of the course are paired with specific readings that illustrate the key points, all in the same book. Often the readings come from standard journals; sometimes they are written just for the book.

There is a potential for some income in writing textbooks. If picked up by a large number of your colleagues and assigned to their students, sales could be in the thousands or tens of thousands of copies, rather than the hundreds. Some of the most successful textbook authors have quit their academic jobs just to write more books. But there is also a catch. Textbooks need to be revised to maintain this flow of income. As the number of used copies increase in the marketplace, new editions are needed to renew the income for both the publisher and the author. So, after you take the year out of your life to write Introduction to Qualitative Research, plan on doing it all over again in a couple of years. If nobody buys the book and nobody cares, you've wasted that year on a lost book. If they do like it, you might be rewriting that book every three or four years for a very long time.

Supplemental Texts. Everything else that can get used in a college course, from freshman to graduate level, can be considered a supplemental text. They are called "supplemental" textbooks because they are not designed to provide the core information for a class but to enrich that knowledge in some fashion. Some supplemental texts cover one of the themes or subjects of a course. Some are research studies expanded to show the relevance of the study to the broad literature in that area. Some are books of case studies. Some introduce methodology or theory. Authors here generally write their own book for their own purposes and, magically, some of their colleagues value the content of the book enough to assign it for a class. Publishers will steer authors in this direction with their professional writing. If you can get a colleague to demand a class of students buy your book, the sales are much larger and the long-term impact greater. From the publisher's standpoint, it is crucial that you not only report what you found in your study, but provide the context of it in terms of the broader field or in terms of the Big Question you are asking. These text-like elements can transform writing about your research into a teachable product.

What About Editing a Book?

You and your posse show up at the qualitative conference in Urbana. Everyone agreed to sit on the panel you organized on new materialism or qualitative rigor or the ethnography of hospices. The atmosphere in the room is electric. Each paper is better than the one before and everyone is nodding their head as the next speaker gets up. What a great set of papers! At the end, over beer at Murphy's Pub down the street, everyone agrees that this session should get published as a book. You volunteer to be the editor. After putting together your proposal and shopping it around to various potential publishers (see chapter 6 for how to do that), you are stunned that none of them is interested. What happened? As you relay the bad news to your colleagues and friends, there comes back the refrain, "Yeah, I've heard that publishers don't like edited books."

To a large extent, that rap is true. Publishers tend not to like edited volumes. A brief look at their sales figures will tell you why. (No, they won't really show you their sales figures, this is all hypothetical.) Edited books, as a group, tend to perform more poorly than authored ones. You could have discerned this from your own buying pattern. When you see an edited book of interest, your decision usually is made only after reviewing the table of contents. If 10 of the 12 chapters are of interest, you're likely to buy it. But what if only six are? Or three? In most cases, you'll pass on the opportunity and hope your library picks the book up so you can copy or scan or download the couple of chapters you really want. Or pick them off of Academia.edu. The publisher gets only a few library sales that way, rarely enough to financially support the work.

Why do you usually only find a couple of chapters in an edited book to be of interest? Edited volumes, particularly ones that emanate from conferences, tend to be a scattering of individualized papers held together by a cover. Some will be broad and theoretical, some narrowly carved case studies, some dense with data, others thoughtful essays. Some are written with general audiences in mind, others framed to cater to only a few specialists, some a rehash of what the writer did for a journal last month. Who would want a book like that? There is no blame to be assigned here, but each individual author writes her paper in her own style for her own purpose to her own audience. Some of your colleagues can talk better than they write. Some can hardly write at all. Some don't have English as their first language, and putting things on paper in Korean won't help you much. Some don't have the time to do as thorough a job as you would like. That's a collection of papers, not a book. And that electricity that was in the room when you were all delivering those papers—even if all were good ones—doesn't hold when they are put down in black and white two years after the event. Publishers have too often been convinced by the enthusiasm of a volume editor and taken the chance, only to find out that the general rule of edited books holds true once again. Publishers say no because we've been burned too often by saying yes.

The advice here seems to be to give a pass to any edited volumes. When your panel mates oooh and aaah over the exquisite quality of the papers, just tell them, "We'll put them in a journal." Not a bad thought. As we discussed above, there are plenty of journals out there. One of them might like a thematic issue on the topic of your session.

You can go about an edited book another way. If the problem with edited books is that the papers are written by many people for many reasons in many styles, a well-ordered and designed volume might be able to fix some of that. Forget you ever had that session. Forget all your friends' papers. Open a blank file and design this book the way you think it should be written, as if you were writing it yourself. Fill in the outline of the book you would ideally write. Then find which of your panel participants (or others not associated with your session) would be able to write each chapter better than you could. Invite them to contribute; give them explicit instructions on what you want them to write and what audience they are writing for. Ignore your friends who can't write their way out of a paper bag and the ones whom you know never deliver on time. This kind of edited book can sometimes work; the one designed by one or two people who bully all their contributors to write pieces the way the editors want them to, covering what the editors want them to cover. You may actually get an edited volume that is well designed, written for a single audience with a set of harmonic voices. This is the kind of edited book you would want to read.

Two other considerations here. If your topic is identical to or part of the curriculum of a common course in your discipline, this edited book could serve as one of those supplemental texts that sells far better than other books, because it can be assigned to students as a reader for that course as well as being bought by fellow researchers. Also, if the book is the first foray into a new, upcoming research area, one in which no single individual knows enough to write the book him or herself but many people want to know the "state of the art," those kinds of edited books often are successful. But that's not most of the edited volumes submitted to me and to other publishers.

Let's go back one step. "Edit their pieces heavily." "Follow up regularly." Why those instructions? Because of the other dirty secret of editing a book—it's no fun. Rather than engaging your contributors in deep intellectual discussions about their contributions, more often your role is that of a cat herder.

- George really can't write; his ghost writer got her degree last year and no longer edits his papers for him. That's your job now.
- Amir is doing field work in Burkina Faso for the next 12 weeks and will have internet access only twice in his field season. He'll try to get his piece done, but no promises.
- Maria has to put together her tenure packet by June 30 and can't get to her paper until after that.
- Max turned in a paper that obviously ignored the explicit instructions you gave him. "Instructions?" he asks.
- Whitney lost her father and is embroiled with lawyers and estates.

And so on. My experience is that, on average, about a quarter of your contributors will deliver on time, at the required length, with the content and writing style you requested. That only leaves another eight authors that you have to track down and get them to deliver the goods, good goods. Your job as the editor will be to listen to all the excuses while pretending to be sympathetic, beg/cajole/threaten your contributors to turn their pieces in, edit their pieces, give them instructions for rewriting, or rewrite the chapter yourself. You will discover your colleagues have ego issues and neuroses you never knew about.

If there are any effective strategies for the editorial cat-herding process, they involve communication and modeling. Set out a schedule from the beginning that all contributors are expected to follow. Send periodic reminders of upcoming deadlines, imminent deadlines, and deadlines just past. Authors who know that you are serious about having them deliver in a specific time frame are more likely to do so. If the rest of the contributors have already submitted their papers, the delinquent author is more likely to put it higher on his priority list. An edited volume will move only as swiftly as its slowest contributor. Try to identify who that will be and spend the greatest part of your effort getting that contributor to deliver on time. Conduct yourself in the same fashion. If you expect contributors to turn around revisions in two weeks, make sure that your editing of their revisions is equally timely. If you've asked them to limit their length to 20 pages, don't write 35 yourself.

Sadly, you also need to be prepared to let go. Some contributors are unlikely to ever deliver the chapter. Or they are unable write it in the style you have requested of them or cover the content you expected. It is not uncommon that the final manuscript delivered to the publisher does not contain the same set of articles you originally promised.

If you are enough of a bully, give firm and explicit instructions of what you want, edit pieces heavily, and follow up regularly, you may end up with a good edited book. But, from my experience, that is the exception rather than the rule. Often you would have been better served just writing the damned thing yourself.

Researching Potential Publishers

Having decided the kind of book you wish to write, how do you go about finding the right publisher? The answer here will be abbreviated, because it is the identical process as was described for finding the right journal for your article in chapter 3. Like the journal process, you should do this work before you invest the time in writing your book.

Just as you will do a literature search before beginning to do fieldwork, you should gather information on potential publishers from available sources as a crucial preliminary step.

First, build your bibliography. In this case, look on your bookshelf to see which publishers' books regularly appear there. It is likely that those presses have an interest in your subject. Similarly, keep flyers you receive from different publishers over a period of time. Check who regularly attends conferences or advertises in journals in your discipline. If you and your colleagues are not on a publisher's mailing list and are not included as part of its advertising or conference budget, it is less likely that press reaches the audience for your book effectively than a publisher who regularly advertises to you and people like yourself.

Next, start networking and interviewing informants—colleagues, mentors, people who have previously published with a press you are interested in, series editors for that press. Many of your colleagues have had dealings with publishers and have information that may be of value. Even if their data is anecdotal, these people may be able to provide you with contacts into the network of acquisitions editors who will decide whether or not to publish your book.

How important is it to getting published to have contact with an editor? A study done in the 1970s by Walter Powell, a sociologist at Stanford University, demonstrated that, while manuscripts submitted over the transom to a scholarly press had a 0.5 percent chance of being accepted for publication, those odds increased to 8 percent for someone who had some prior contact with the press, and 35 percent when directly solicited by the editor (Powell 1985, p. 169).

Identifying Your Goals

As with your journal article, understanding what you want from getting a book published is crucial in identifying the right publisher. Those goals could include:

- Money. Who will pay the largest amount in royalties or advances? (see chapter 8)
- Aesthetics. Whose books do you find the most attractive?
- Prestige. Which publishing house will be most favorably regarded for tenure or promotion decisions?
- Advertising and Distribution. Which press will most aggressively sell the book to your colleagues?
- Pricing. Who will price it in such a way that they or their students can best afford to buy it?
- Speed of publication. Who will have the book in the hands of readers the quickest?
- Specific markets. If there are specific groups of people for whom you are writing, which press best reaches those groups?

No one publisher does *all* of those things better than other publishers. So it is worthwhile to rank these elements, and other considerations you have, in order of importance, then focus on publishers who meet your most important criteria.

This prioritization might also help you shape your topic, since certain goals fit better with certain types of publishers. If the key goal of your publishing a book is to help you get tenure, then you might look toward a university press and design your topic around their interests. If, on the other hand, you're hoping for a large advance to buy that cabin in Maine, then you should think more about writing a textbook and conceptualize your writing project accordingly.

Fieldwork

By now you should be ready to enter the field in your publisher search. You have selected a niche and a topic appropriate for that niche. You have a developed a list of potential publishers who work in your area. You have narrowed that list to the most likely publishing houses, using information garnered from your colleagues and from your own observations on how they advertise and what they've published in the past.

If your network has provided you with an informant inside a publishing house, use it. If not, you may have to enter without help, as you would in a field project. In either case, your background research is never a substitute for direct work in the field. So contact publishers on your short list and get some first-hand data.

The person with whom you wish to speak is, most often, the acquisitions editor for your discipline. Your research should have turned up this person's name, email, and some understanding of her behavioral habits. The acquisitions editor is the gatekeeper in most publishing houses, the person who recommends publication of your book to the press's publications board, who has to answer to the house for its success or failure, who shepherds it through the development and production process, and who champions the project among jaded marketing directors, color-blind cover designers, and abacus-wielding accountants. The editor also is likely to be your best informant about the press. Depending on your preferred style of interaction, you can reach the editor by email, phone, or face-to-face at national conferences, which most editors regularly attend. Editors also regularly visit many university campuses and so can be encountered on your home turf.

As with most interviews, questions will emerge from the discussion. But there are some structured starting points that I've outlined in Table 5.2.

The skillful interviewer can often induce the editor to compare her press with others on your list or can elicit the names of her counterparts at other presses. This is particularly useful if she indicates that the book is not appropriate for her press. She can give you the next lead in your publishing search. Like the journal editor, the acquiring editor may also get involved in shaping your project to specifically fit the press's needs, making her sponsorship, and therefore publication, more likely.

Your interview should give you a good idea of the level of enthusiasm the editor has for your project and its likelihood to be accepted by this press. You also will get a sense of her personal style. If things don't click between you, remember that you might be working with her for years and must place a lot of trust in her to handle your book throughout the process. Do you feel comfortable enough to commit to that long-term relationship?

In the next chapter, we will translate your budding relationship with an acquisitions editor into a book proposal that she couldn't possibly turn down.

Table 5.2 Interview Questions for the Acquisition Editor

- ► What are the strengths of the press?
- ► What are its customary procedures and timetable for reviewing submitted proposals or manuscripts?
- ► How long should a manuscript be?
- ► What are the standard terms of a contract?
- ► What are their standard practices and timetable for producing a book?
- ► How do they price and market books? What audiences do they reach and how do they reach them?
- ► What is the nature and focus of their list in your field?
- ► After you describe your project, can the editor tell you how likely the press is to be interested in your book? What would make it more appealing?
- ► What information do they need to make a publication decision?

Chapter 6

The Book Proposal

You've identified a list of publishers who are desirable for your book. You've paved the way with discussions with the editor at that press and know how you will approach writing the book in a way that press will find attractive. But without a contract to publish the book, you are looking at a long writing assignment with no guaranteed payoff. To get that contract, the editor has asked you for a book proposal. Their website has a set of guidelines to use. I'll help you through the unspoken subtext of those guidelines so you can make your book idea look impressive to all who read it.

When we discussed journals, I suggested that you start with an abstract and title. The same holds true when you're ready to write your book: create a title and a book proposal, which is an abstract on steroids, and send it to the publishers of your choice. This is what any acquisitions editor will want to see from you to begin the discussion that you will have with her. As with a journal article, this is the place to start, not to labor over your manuscript for a year and send it off into cyberspace in the hopes that the editor will read all 423 closely argued pages and 118 supporting tables.

I once had an anthropologist friend visit me in my office while I was finishing my last activity for the week: going through that week's accumulated pile of manuscripts and proposals to find the ones that we would look at further. There was only one or two of the 20 in the stack that passed this first filter. What horrified her was that I ran through the entire stack in the span of 10 minutes. Most of the decisions were made before I finished reading the first page of the proposal. The full manuscripts got about the same amount of attention. Yes, putting together a good proposal is *that* important.

Writing a decent book proposal is not easy. After all, you assume that it will be read by informed colleagues who will want answers to questions about how you are addressing a topic of great interest to them. But the proposal will be read first by the acquiring editor at the press, who may be academically trained in fourteenth century English literature or liquid flow engineering and knows nothing of your subject area. So you have to both dumb down and muscle up to two different readers. Not an easy task. But it is a good gauge of how well you can write, one of the key factors in your publisher deciding to do your book.

What belongs in the proposal are items for both of those readers. Both are interested in the intellectual content and approach you are taking. The editor is also interested in more mundane things—how long a manuscript is it going to be, when are you going to send in a full draft, how many illustrations. She is also very interested in one less mundane item: who is going to buy it.

A prospectus should consist of six parts. In some cases, publishers will have a specific proposal format in order to ensure they have all of this information. If not, you should still look at the guidelines for the publisher to whom you are submitting the proposal; that information will be on their website. The length can vary, but a good rule of thumb is no more than five pages for the proposal. Accompanying material like a sample chapter and CV will be longer, but might not get read if the proposal is not compelling.

Part 1: What Is Your Book About?

This is your abstract. It should run no more than one to two pages. It should be sophisticated enough that your colleagues will understand its importance, but jargon-free and sufficiently contextualized that the acquisitions editor will also understand why your book is important. That's key. The book is not just a data dump of the key elements of your study. Show how your book is important, important enough that people will want to shell out good money to read it, that libraries will consider it essential to put on their shelves, and that the publisher will want to put it up for book awards. So don't be shy. Tell the editor and reviewers what you are doing that no one else has ever done. "This is the first book to…" is not a bad way to start a paragraph. You don't need to fully examine all the literature in these one or two pages, but cite who your primary inspirations are. And explain what a reader will get out of the book.

You will want to comment on your methodological and theoretical approach, the level of complexity of the ideas and the writing, the types of data you have to support your ideas, and the topics you plan to cover. If based on a study, give a brief description of it. In this way, it is not different from the article abstract discussed in chapter 3.

Part 2: Who Is Going to Buy It?

This part of the prospectus is usually the hardest one for the scholar to write, yet is the most important piece to the publisher. You need to know for whom you are writing the book and be able convey that information to the publisher in the most detailed manner possible. That information allows the publisher to make a calculated guess as to the size of the market.

Shouldn't the publisher already know all this? Well, yes and no. If you've done your homework right, you've picked a publisher who is familiar with your field. But each field is a vast array of smaller scholarly communities, and the publisher won't know all of them, will certainly not know your subfields as well as you do. If your work extends beyond a single discipline, the publisher may not be aware of those external audiences either.

What kind of information is the publisher looking for? The average professor's answer is: "This book will be of use to scholars in my field, their graduate and undergraduate students, scholars and students in the related fields of x, y, and z, and the informed public." Useless. The number of books that have that breadth of reach is about zero.

What is useful is specific information and specialized knowledge that you have but the publisher might not. In drafting this section of your book proposal, try to answer the questions below. And think of your audience as a set of ever wider circles. The few specialists in your network are your most likely purchasers. If you write the book the way you hope to, the broader discipline, the students of the discipline, secondary markets in related fields might also be attracted for various reasons. Far off in the distance, you even hope that your book sells outside the academy to a general public. Very far off. Don't pick out your Mercedes based on the anticipated royalties from sales to a broad public. Few academic books ever get there.

Let's start with your core audience. Who are they? No, it's not all qualitative researchers, who range from arts-based Buddhist poets to hard-grinding mixed method health evaluators. Where on the continuum does your crowd fit? And more important, how do they talk to each other, for the publisher is going to insinuate herself into that conversation to mention your book to this audience.

What organizations do they belong to? What subsections of those organizations? What listservs do they use? Yahoo groups? Journals they read? Newsletters? Conferences they attend? Specifically, small specialized conferences? Can you help gauge how many people there are in this scholarly community? What do they teach? How many students do their courses have? If this sounds like a research job, it is. It's researching your own community of practice so that the publisher can find the most effective channels to reach them. If you have any knowledge of those information channels, don't hide it from your potential publisher.

How do you find all this information? Like with researching journals, much of it is around you. What journals do *you* read? Conferences you attend? Classes you teach? Listservs you are on? Quantifying these into sizes of audience is not as hard as you think. Professional organizations will have a roster of members of their sections or special interest groups. Listserv owners can tell you how many lurkers there are on their list. Conference organizers know how many people show up each year. It's a matter of asking a few questions, the kind of questions a researcher knows how to ask.

Most universities, government, and research organizations have a publicity office. Will they help announce your book? How about the alumni publications of the schools you received your degrees from?

Mailing lists? Look at your own professional email address book. Look in your files for the address list of workshop attendees at that fun gathering in New Orleans last year. The contact list of the encyclopedia

Table 6.1 Marketing Information Needed in the Book Proposal

- ▶ Scholarly organizations, including sections and special interest groups
- ▶ Journals, newsletters
- ▶ Conferences, national, regional, and specialized
- ▶ Personal mailing lists and lists accumulated from your previous activities
- ▶ Courses, name and level, core or supplemental text
- ▶ Listservs, blogs, and other web groups
- ▶ Social media accounts, personal website, or blog
- ▶ Your organization's publicity office
- ▶ Group sales
- ▶ Local events

you contributed to a while back. You have lots of information on potential buyers that your publisher can use. Find it.

Start building your own mailing list database of people you know are interested in your work. All those people who send you an email asking questions about one of your papers they have read. All those students who have attended your seminars. That list is golden to your publisher. It also shows you to be a savvy academic able to help the publisher market your work.

In the contemporary electronically mediated world, more and more the publishers want to know who the electronic gatekeepers are. Bloggers, Facebook and Yahoo groups, rabid tweeters. Do you have a blog? Do you know any bloggers personally? Or do you have a friend who has a friend who once dated...

How do you know how many people teach the courses your book is designed for? There are organizations that collect and sell that data to publishers who are hungry for it. Look online for the MDR higher ed catalog,[1] which pulls information from major textbook publishers and their field reps. You can browse the summary data online. Another service, PubTrack, owned by Nielsen Market Research, pulls information from college bookstores on which book is used for which class. Many publishers subscribe to this, though you will have difficulty accessing it without a subscription. Or, if you have the time and willingness (or a research assistant), you can manually compile a list of people who teach the class for which your book is geared from various university websites. Some professional organizations collect syllabi for different classes on their website to help you.

In addition to the course name, level and, if you're lucky, the number of instructors, it is also useful to the publisher to know if your book is designed as a main text for this course or as a supplemental one. How many students does this course usually attract? Even if you can't gather this information nationally or internationally, you certainly can offer it about your campus and those of your network of friends.

As you move from your core audience to your wider discipline and neighboring disciplines, the research gets harder. You don't know those people as well. But you are a good qualitative researcher, and it would only take a couple of phone calls or emails, or a cup of coffee with a colleague down the hall, to elicit this kind of information from your few colleagues who are in those neighboring fields. You're looking for the same kinds of information here: main organizations, sub-groups within organizations, newsletters, journals, listservs, web groups, blogs, Facebook pages, and so forth.

One criterion to examine is the level of sophistication at which you have pegged your work. If the book is to be written for your professional colleagues, the proposal will spend much less time on the context of your field and much more on the detailed arguments between specialists. If it is designed for beginning master's qualitative methods students, your outline probably needs a section introducing the basic principles of grounded theory, not simply a discussion of the differences in memo-writing strategies between Strauss, Glaser, and Charmaz. You need to tell your publisher that's where you're pegging your book.

A final category of useful information comes under the category of special sales. While few academic publishers rely on bookstore sales, setting up a book signing event in your local bookstore is not uncommon. Are there groups who might make a bulk purchase so the publisher can sell a bunch at the same time?

Once you get a publisher to agree to publish your book, don't throw this information away. When the manuscript is submitted, you will undoubtedly be hit with a marketing questionnaire, asking you these questions all over again. If your information is up to date, that document will be easy to compile (see chapter 10).

Part 3: How Are You Qualified to Write It?

What experience, background or other qualifications do you bring to the project that uniquely qualifies you to undertake it? Answer this question in a paragraph. Make it a good paragraph and, as above, don't be shy about demonstrating your expertise on this topic. If you have trouble tooting your own horn, have your best friend write this section for you. Attach a current abbreviated CV. You don't need to include the names of all your graduate students or of all the university committees you've served on but anything relevant to your book in your teaching, research, and writing should be included. Awards, media exposure, and important positions in professional organizations are good. If the book has numerous contributors, include their current affiliations and a very brief description of each of their qualifications. Make yourself look good, the publisher will want to portray you as a famous, brilliant scholar to sell your book. Give them reasons to do so.

Part 4: What Is It Going to Look Like?

Here's where you add all the mundane details of length, format, delivery date. Make sure you include all of this information. The publisher really does need to know it.

Length. In this age of variable fonts, best to offer this information in number of words. Figure 300 words on a Times Roman 12 double spaced manuscript page. Thus, if you have a 200 double-spaced page manuscript, estimate 60,000 words. But you haven't written the book yet. How do you know how long it is going to be? Look at your proposed table of contents. If your chapters run about the same length as an academic article (30 manuscript pages=9,000 words) and you have nine chapters plus a bibliography, you should estimate 90,000 words (9,000 words x 10 chapters). Length matters to a publisher. They have to publish all those words. The longer it goes, the more expensive to produce. In your networking with the publisher, you should find out what their expected range of manuscript lengths is. For Left Coast, it's 40,000–100,000 words. But it could be different for another press.

Current status. If there are some chapters done, let the editor know, both the number of chapters ready to show and the approximate length of each.

Timetable for completing the rest. If you thought calculating the length gave you headaches, try estimating writing time. The publisher can't do this for you, nor do you want them to. So sit down and coldly analyze your writing speed. How many articles did you really finish last year? How many are you committed to this year? If you typically write three articles a year, don't promise the publisher you'll finish a nine chapter book in six months. And that's not taking into account the unexpected appointment as graduate admissions director, the week you lost when your kid got very sick (I'm sorry, hope he's better now), the obligatory piece for your mentor's festschrift that you weren't planning on, your course load, fieldwork season, the departmental accreditation report you got stuck writing, the two week cruise to Alaska with your aged aunt, and so forth. If someone tells me that it will take less than twelve months, I'm skeptical unless they are on sabbatical and locked in a cabin without internet access for half of that time. If they promise a date over two years away, I'm suspicious that they don't really have a writing schedule. But only you know how much writing time you will have available and how diligent you will be in using it.

Reviewers. As with a journal article, it is certainly acceptable—and often helpful to the editor—to suggest qualified reviewers and, if necessary, people who should not review the book.

Illustrations. Are there tables, figures, maps, photographs or other non-text material to be included? Approximately how many of each? Do they need to be in color? Are there other aural or visual elements required, things that cannot go into a printed book but might be included in an eBook? Each publisher will have their own policy with non-textual materials, preferred number of illustrations, color printing, digital files. You can find out their practices when you network with the editor.

Headaches. Are there other technical problems the publisher should be aware of? For example, figures that won't reduce to the publisher's standard page size, permissions needed to reprint copyrighted material, restrictions placed upon you by granting agencies, your own non-negotiable contract demands.

Part 5: What Else Is Out There?

Yes, of course, your book really has no "competitor." It's uniquely you and your research, thinking, and writing. But if no one has ever written on this topic before, the publisher is likely to think that there is no one else working on it. How will they sell copies if no one else is interested in your topic? Find the closest competing books and include citations. Then briefly analyze how your book will be better and/or different from them. Be careful with this analysis. If you are very critical of one of the competitors and that author reviews your proposal, it might come back to hurt you. It always helps to include a best seller in your area. Publishers are often lured to the hope of duplicating that success. This is particularly true if your book is designed as a textbook or has use in a specific course.

Part 6: Your Writing Sample

Here's the rubber-road nexus. Can you actually write? Don't just send a journal article that you wrote under duress. It won't show your writing capabilities at their best. Nor will sending the introduction to the book you are writing. Most of that information is already in the prospectus you have just finished. Pull out a section that gives the reader the level of sophistication and the level of background knowledge needed, and shows off your style. Prove to the publisher that you can pull off the job if they say yes. After all, agreeing to publish a book is going to cost them megabucks. I usually quote the figure $20,000 to potential authors; it's pretty close. Wouldn't you want some kind of assurance that the project will turn out well if you were investing that amount of money?

How Publishers Make Decisions

When we discussed journals, I emphasized the socially constructed nature of the decision-making process by journal editors. The same applies here, only the stakes are higher. In the case of a journal, the contents are already paid for by libraries or by your association membership dues. In the case of a book, the publisher is investing real money in you and your ideas and hoping for a return. Trust really matters—trust that your ideas are good, that you can write, that you will deliver what you say you will when you say you will. And trust comes from social interaction.

That trust, as much as your ideas, will drive the acquiring editor at the publishing house, for there is usually a large amount of leeway in her decision making. Every publisher has a set of idealized book ideas that they think are "winners." If you're lucky enough to have a book in mind that fits that profile, they'll snatch it up quickly. There is a whole set of book projects that the press is sure they don't want—books that are too narrowly constructed to succeed, books that are geared to fields that the press doesn't market to, books that are designed for audience sectors that the press doesn't reach. That leaves the middle ground of books that fit the list but aren't guaranteed winners. And those are the ones the editor chooses among. Those books will rarely have an obvious upside, the markings of best sellers, though some will become those. They also are not likely to lose money, because of the publisher's experience of the level of sales of similar projects. The editor's decisions of which book ideas to champion among the many that have been submitted might be driven by an interesting idea, an interesting approach, recent discussions with some of your colleagues that a certain research area is growing in popularity, or a similar book that was very successful. It also might be driven by her belief in you and your ideas. If you've had conversations with this editor, you should have some idea of what is driving her interest in your book idea.

This becomes important because the editor's initial review of your proposal, her choice of reviewers for feedback, and the passion with which she approaches her publications board with a recommendation to publish your book depend on her level of trust in you and your work—trust that has come from the interactions you have had with her.

Publication Board? The recommendation of your editor, the reviews she has obtained to support her recommendation, and the budget she provides for the potential financial success of the book (remember the list of competing books and length estimates in your proposal?) all go up the chain of command. Different publishers have different approval systems. A university press almost always has a Publications Board made up of faculty at the university. A large commercial press will usually involve the Editorial Director and Marketing Director in approving the recommendation of the editor; sometimes higher level administrators also get involved. At a smaller, commercial press like Left Coast, the editor might only have to convince the publisher to write that $20,000 check.

What are the criteria used? Academic worth of the idea. Reputation of the author. Sales potential. Close fit with the press's current list of titles. Potential for upside sales. And, finally, the editor's passion for the project, which is inseparable from her passion for you and your ideas. Relationships matter.

Multiple Submissions

Can I submit the proposal to more than one press? Unlike the refined game of journal publication, books are a market driven entity. Absolutely, submit your proposal to more than one press! Some university presses, and occasionally others, will insist on an exclusive consideration. That's not unreasonable. Because they're university presses, they feel obligated to fully review every proposal that comes through the door, unlike commercial presses, who can focus on only the ones they really want to pursue. If a university press is the top press on your list of priorities, there's no reason not to try them first—even exclusively. But negotiate a timeline with them. Pick a time frame, probably between three and six months. If they don't have an answer for you in that frame of time, you have the right to withdraw or seek additional publication outlets.

A friend of mine once put together a book on body image, long ago when it was a new hot topic. She sent it to a university press and, after the initial enthusiasm, found it impossible to get any word on the process of consideration from them. A full year went by. She came to me for help, though it wasn't a topic we were interested in publishing at the time (in retrospect, that was a dumb decision on my part. Look what happened to that area!). Together she and I developed a list of a dozen other potential presses, to whom she sent letters of inquiry a few weeks before the major national convention, asking to meet at the conference. She got nine favorable responses, met with six press editors at the conference, and had three book contract offers within a month after the conference.

If a publisher really wants your book and knows other presses are also considering it, they'll work harder and faster to get you an answer, hopefully a favorable answer in the form of a contract offer, to snatch this desirable project away from the competition.

Literary Agents

Do you need an agent? Literary agents were once a standard fixture in the publishing industry. They still are in trade publishing, so if you're writing a book for a popular audience, you need to pay attention to them. They serve as the intermediaries between authors and publishers. Those publishers are always flooded with Hemingway wannabes. Every publisher's office has a corner with the slush pile, given to an intern to wade through and find a project or two out of the hundreds submitted that the overworked editor should pay attention to. The agent serves the same function, weeding out the golden nuggets from the chaff (sorry about the mixed metaphor). She brings those few she thinks are worthwhile to the editor to consider. She will also scour her list of potential publishers to find the right ones for a particular project she takes on, will advocate for the author, negotiate contracts for the author, and keep an eye on the project throughout the publication and marketing process. The agent usually tries to sell paperback and electronic rights, movie rights, article excerpts to magazines, and other ways of monetizing your work. In exchange the author pays her a percentage of the royalties earned on the book, usually 10–15 percent.

But note that this has made getting a publisher to say yes a two-step process. First, you have to convince the agent, and then the agent still has to convince a publisher to invest in your book. In the cutthroat trade book world, that might be a worthwhile tradeoff. In scholarly or textbook publishing, there's rarely a benefit to using an agent. Publisher's royalties are generally fixed, their publication programs are focused in specific areas, their sales upside is usually limited—are you giving away a share to your agent without a good reason? Most academic book contracts are negotiated without the benefit of an agent.

Final Reminders

The function of the book proposal is to sell a specific press on your idea. Tailor your proposal to the interests of the editor who will make the decision, the reviewers who are likely to examine it for the editor, and the publications board that has to approve the editor's decision. Having already spoken to that editor to ascertain her interests, you should have some idea of how to present the ideas. If you are submitting to several presses, feel free to vary the proposals to each one, highlighting what you think would interest that press. If you are unclear on how to present your proposal, call the editor again for guidance. This will also remind the editor that the proposal is coming soon, will build your relationship with her, will help focus your proposal to her interests. She is more likely to give your proposal her attention than the others that come in that day's mail.

Reiterating the key point of this book: editorial decision making is not a science, it is socially constructed. The publisher's decision, just like the journal editor's, is based on a variety of factors, many of which have little to do with the quality of the ideas or of the writing. The manner in which you present your proposal, and your relationship with the editor who is reviewing it, can make an enormous difference in whether or not you are offered a publishing contract. If, after conversations with the editor, you are on good terms, that gives her reasons to trust you will deliver what you promise in the proposal. The decision to say yes becomes easier when trust has been built.

Nor will all publishers view the same idea in the same way. As with a journal article, if one publisher says no, revise the proposal, using whatever useful feedback you received, and try another publisher. If the idea is a good one and your research on appropriate publishers is solid, you're likely to find a publisher for your book.

Chapter 7

Writing the Damn Thing

If you've flipped to this chapter first, you must be desperate. To ask a publisher rather than an accomplished writer for advice on writing is not the best idea. If you want to learn how to write, put this book down and go order a copy of the qualitative writing books by Laurel Richardson, Harry Wolcott, Bud Goodall, or Howie Becker. Details are in appendix A. Those folks really know how to write and can teach you how to write good qualitative prose far better than I can.

But, before you move to another chapter, let me tell you what I can help you with: the mechanical stuff of getting started, keeping going, reaching closure. This is the stuff that an experienced editor (and ersatz psychologist) can offer so that you can focus on making that prose deathless rather than worrying whether you'll get a word on paper before your death. If that's what you want, read on.

Oh, and I do have suggestions about how to write well, mostly cribbed from the people mentioned above. But they're abbreviated and derivative. If you want the real stuff, look at those books. Or look at other books written by real writers about writing. Join a writing group. Find a group of tough but sympathetic reviewers. Engage a committed, sympathetic editor. And, most of all, WRITE!

Essentials of Publishing Qualitative Research by Mitchell Allen.
89–110. © 2016 Left Coast Press, Inc. All rights reserved.

Getting Started

Not everyone is like my friend Brian Fagan, an archaeologist who writes uninterruptedly for several hours every morning. He's written about 50 books, if you don't count new editions of his textbooks, some of which are now in edition 12 or 13. Few can match Arthur Asa Berger, who will discuss a book idea with me over dim sum on San Francisco's Clement Street and submit a draft to me three weeks later. I think he's up to about 95 books now.

Let's talk about the rest of us mortals.

Brian's advice consists of a single word: *Write*!!! Write regularly and often. Get into the habit of it. If not your article, write a blog, a diary entry, a shopping list. He sets aside a specific time each day, locks himself into his office with his cats, turns off his email, and doesn't emerge until his writing time is up (Fagan 2010, p. 203).

The late Bud Goodall (2008, p. 60), one of qual research's all-time best writers, offered much the same advice: "First rule of writing: Write every day... As is true with any other skill, it requires regular disciplined practice."

You might not have Brian's discipline, but *every* book about writing ever published will tell you the same thing. The only way to be a writer is to write. So, put this book down, sidle over to your computer, and write 200 words before you move on to the next paragraph here. If you need a writing prompt, write about how all the advice about writing is bullshit and you really don't have the time to write every day. Get going on that one and 200 words will be a snap. Maybe you should stop when you hit 1,000.

[A pause in the action while you write something.]

...Now that you're back, with your 1,000 pissed-off words done, was that so bad? A thousand words equals about two single-spaced pages. Think of all the angry memos to your department chair or the facilities department you've dashed off like that. The long letters you wrote to an editor explaining why your manuscript is late (I have a few of the better ones framed on my wall). If you can churn out 1,000 words in a day—just two pages—here's the result.

- An average academic article of 6,000–8,000 words will be done in a week!
- A brief academic book of 50,000 words like this one (200 double-spaced pages) will be done in less than two months. You'd even get a week off for Mardi Gras in New Orleans and still get it done on time.

Just 1,000 words a day. That's all it takes. Half a dozen memos to your department chair and you have an article. Half a dozen articles (they're called chapters in the book trade) and you have a book. If you can't write 1,000 words some days,

write 500

or write 100

or write 50

or write one sentence

...but write something, even if you eventually decide to throw it away. The editing process, which we will discuss later in this chapter, is not the same as the writing process. You need words on paper (or in a computer file) to start. As novelist Jodi Picoult states, "You might not write well every day, but you can always edit a bad page. You can't edit a blank page" (www.goodreads.com/quotes/568141-you-can-always-edit-a-bad-page-you-can-t-edit).

Being an archaeologist by training, I've delved into the origins of writing. Our discipline's best guess is that it began in Mesopotamia and may go back to as early as 8,000 or 9,000 years ago (Schmandt-Besserat 1996). The original messages were even shorter and cuter than Twitter posts, little clay tokens that represented goods to be exchanged. Sheep. Cattle. Sheaves of wheat. Emoticons of the Neolithic. But these tokens seemed to get lost when transported from one

Zagros mountain village to another, so they were put in hollow clay balls to keep them intact. The problem with clay envelopes was a lack of plastic windows, so you couldn't see how many tokens were inside and whether they were sheep or sheaves. The enterprising merchant would inscribe a picture of the nature and quantity of the tokens on the outside of this clay ball with a triangular tool now called a stylus.

Eventually, some genius realized that, if you had the number and nature of the objects on the clay ball, you didn't really need the tokens inside at all. So he flattened the ball into a small tablet and just inscribed the information on the tablet with his stylus. Over time, this pictographic system evolved into dozens of little scratch marks into the clay, by hand. Hence, cuneiform writing. Complex literary and legal texts, like the Epic of Gilgamesh and Hammurabi's Code came a lot later. The alphabet was a late addition, about 1500 BC.

Now please stop complaining about how slow your computer is. You could be trying to finish your article on a clay tablet with a stylus!

When Should You Start Writing?

Yesterday. Well, given the nature of the space-time continuum, let's settle for today.

I was puzzled when Harry Wolcott (2009, pp. 20, 22) wrote in *Writing Up Qualitative Research*, "You cannot begin writing early enough… Write a preliminary draft of the study. Then begin the research." But now I find his logic inescapable. You already know a lot about your topic. You've written an abstract of your article or a proposal for your book. That's all part of your final text. You have ideas about your theoretical foundation; you have a clear sense about what methods you will use; you've already read some of the important literature on the topic and how it will influence your work. You may even have some hint of what conclusions your research might lead you to. Rather than keeping those in abstruse notes, write them down as text. And continue to write text as you proceed with the study: interview notes, summaries of important literature, careful descriptions of the methods you've used, reflections on theoretical ideas that are scrambling your brain. When you're done, you may find your task as author will be to edit down your work rather than write it. It's largely written already.

You might protest that you don't really know what you're writing about that early. That you need clarity before you can "write up" your results. That's not the way it works, according to the best writers in the field:

> Writers come to realize what they believe in the process of writing, in the act of finding the language that crystallizes their thoughts and sentiments. It is a process of "writing into" rather than "writing up" a subject. When writing up a subject, writers know what they wish to say before the composition process begins. When writing into a subject, writers discover what they know through writing. (Pelias 2011, p. 660)

Or, ask Laurel Richardson. She'll tell you, "Writing stories and personal narratives have increasingly become the structures through which I make sense of my world, locating my particular biographical experiences in larger historical and sociological contexts" (Richardson and St. Pierre 2005, p. 966). Even world-renowned writers like Margaret Atwood experience this process of writing as inquiry:

> For me the experience of writing is really an experience of losing control.... I think it's very much like dreaming or like surfing. You go out there and wait for a wave, and when it comes it takes you somewhere and you don't know where it'll go. (therumpus.net/2012/07/margaret-atwood-on-the-internet/)

The sooner you start writing, the sooner you will understand what you're writing about.

Where Do You Start Writing?

A good multiple choice question.

    A) At the beginning

    B) In the middle

    C) At the end

    D) None of the above

My friend C. Deborah Laughton, methodology publisher with Guilford Press who teaches joint workshops on qualitative publishing with me, suggests that you start on what you're dying to say or the topic you could cover in your sleep.

Rephrased: Start with the easiest place of entrée, the place from which you can get launched the quickest. Don't start writing with page 1. Your brain will think it has to have the whole piece figured out and just needs to be transferred to a file. That never happens. Start in the middle, start with some of your descriptive data. Start with something that you know you want to say. You need to write all those words before the whole manuscript is done anyway. Write the easy ones first. They might lead to other easy ones. Save the hard ones, the parts you still haven't figured out, for the days you're ready to tackle them. By the time you get there, it might be clearer what you want to say and how you want to say it. You'll certainly have plenty of text to precede and follow those tough sections by then.

Keeping Going

One of the hardest psychological challenges to overcome is thinking that you have to write the whole thing in one shot. Any document, whether a 25 page article or a 300 page book, is not gonna happen overnight. So find a way of breaking it up into smaller, manageable units.

If you write articles following the typical IMRAD formula—introduction, methods, results, discussion—each unit can be conceptualized and written separately. Look at each unit as a discrete writing assignment. Only put them together at the end. The same theory applies to writing a book. You're writing 8 or 12 separate articles/ chapters. Work on small pieces of chapter 3 for a few days, then chapter 7. Each chapter should be broken up into smaller chunks, the way you would an article. There are just more of them. Eventually, enough pieces of chapter 3 will be done that you can turn it into a complete chapter.

If you're willing to create a detailed outline that breaks the article/ book into 1,000 word chunks, you can decide which chunk you want to tackle on a given day. And decide what you'll tackle tomorrow so you can think about it overnight. These chunks don't need to be written in sequence. They just need to be bite-sized. And written. Some chunks might be pretty vague, "something about new materialist theory." At some point, you'll know what you want to say about it and can write that chunk. It's a lot less intimidating than thinking, "I have to finish my book by April."

All that cogitating is rarely restricted to the section you are writing any given Sunday. You'll think of things you forgot in your methods section while you're writing about theory. Don't stop what you're doing. C. Deborah suggests that you create notes or ideas for each chapter or section and place them in its own file as you think of them; then return to writing the part you're working on. You'll already have some writing prompts when you get around to writing that other section.

One nifty trick: When you stop writing for the day, *leave the last sentence unfinished*. You know your first few words when you pick up where you left off the next day.

The psychological battle is half of it. Don't be brutal on yourself. Be kind. Reward yourself for each accomplishment. I'll go for cookie dough ice cream any time. You undoubtedly have your own favorites. But not until you finish the 1,000 words you promised yourself.

Like your workout regimen, take a day off when you hit a wall… but not too many days or you lose momentum.

When Is Your Manuscript Done?

Forget your perfect offering
There is a crack in everything
That's how the light gets in.

—Leonard Cohen, *Anthem*

There's no way of knowing when you're done. I've had authors who sat on a finished manuscript for months or years until they could tinker with it a bit more to make it "right." It will never be right if you're the only person who has looked at it. So, when all of those sections of text are written, ordered, and arrayed in the file, it's time to send it off.

Well, maybe not quite yet. First, it's time to…

Edit

How many times do you edit your work?

- Edit while you're writing
- Edit your previous day's work
- Edit when you hit a major milestone (a complete section, a complete article or chapter)
- Edit when you think it's done
- Then edit it again

- Then bribe someone who has fresh eyes and good language skills for their edit
- Then edit again
- Lather, rinse, repeat

But there is editing and editing. I have a friend to whom I give most of my work for editing. What comes back is always the same thing—a few typos circled, commas added, word choices questioned. If that's what I'm looking for, she's perfect. But if I want someone to tell me if what I have written makes any sense, I won't get that from her. I have to look elsewhere.

There are numerous levels of editing (Table 7.1). There are certainly other ways of conceiving of it. But dividing the editing task into these different types of tasks allows you to look from the broadest possible standpoint to the narrowest. No single edit of someone's manuscript can do *all* of these. You need to be able to do all of them for any given piece of writing, each at a different pass through your manuscript. Different friends will be able to help you with different types of edits. Each of those friends looks at your work differently. It helps to have a lot of friends. And hopefully you have a couple who are English majors or freelance copyeditors.

Table 7.1: Different Kinds of Editing

- ► Conceptual edit
- ► Structural edit
- ► Content edit
- ► Stylistic edit
- ► Copyedit
- ► Proofreading

- *Conceptual edit.* This is the big picture. Does your article do what you intended? Does it make the point you wanted to make? Does it provide support for your argument? Can someone get through it (an important consideration) and enjoy it? Learn something? Understand why you spent all that time writing it? Understand the importance of what you have to say?

- *Structural edit.* This is one level down in the pyramid of abstraction. You have an argument to present. Does the thesis get presented in the beginning of the piece? Does the evidence supporting your argument sit in the middle and follow in a logical sequence? Do you have a conclusion? Is there a clear roadmap for the reader to know where he is in your argument, what has come before, what comes next? If you were to give your evidence to a jury, would it come back with a conviction? There are templates for structuring an academic article and a dissertation that help you with this step. Did you follow them? If not, does your path take you to the same place?

- *Content edit.* This is one of the things that authors worry about the most. Do you have that interview quote exactly right? Do you cite everyone who ever wrote something on resilience? Do you have the publication dates right in your bibliography? These are the questions to ask of your expert friends, the ones who know your field as well as or better than you do. This allows you to feel safe that the content of what you present is accurate and complete.

- *Stylistic edit.* Academic writing can vary from abstruse and turgid to, well, like, really informal. Yo? Is your style consistent and appropriate for your audience? For this book, a practical guide for advanced students and professionals, I've chosen to write in the first and second person. To talk directly to you. Skip complete sentences, like you would in conversation. That may or may not be appropriate for all academic journals and books. Sometimes, the specific writing of a (re)search tradition like postmodernism calls for unpacking a certain type of nomenclature and stylistic approach. You need to pick a specific style, preferably one appropriate for the publication and your audience, and make sure you keep within it consistently. And each of us has our writing quirks. One publisher I worked for was congenitally incapable of writing a sentence without including a parenthetic phrase (usually unnecessary) in it. I have the bad habit of starting sentences with conjunctions. "And I think..." or "So you should try..." There's at least one of them in this paragraph. Once you know your weak points as a writer, or once one of your friends points out that you use the word "discourse" on every page, take another pass through the manuscript and eliminate as many of these infelicities as you can.

- *Copyedit.* This is where my friend, described above, fits. Right grammar, right punctuation, right words, subject/verb agreement. Completeness and consistency of your references, not only internally but to the APA or Chicago style that you are using. All the stuff you hated in freshman composition. But everyone knows one or two people who were English majors and love telling you when to use "whom" instead of "who." That friend with the useless English degree is finally useful.

- *Proofreading.* A lesser version of the copyedit above. There/their/ they're. Misspelt… or is it misspelled…mispelled…mis…whatever. Incorrectly spelled words.

Six different types of edits. Six passes through the manuscript and a few more to catch what you didn't see the first time. But after a while you stop seeing things. In grounded theory terms, you've reached the point of theoretical saturation. Let's call it "editorial saturation."

Brian Fagan is as efficient an editor as he is a writer. His manuscripts come in pristine and amazingly well written. I convinced him to write me a book about writing archaeology (Fagan 2010) in the vague hope that his exemplary work habits might rub off on some of his dusty colleagues. His suggestions for effective editing would apply here, even if you don't like dirt and don't want to dig for buried treasure. Those solid ideas include:

- Wait several days before editing, so it is fresh
- Have someone read your text aloud to you
- Change margins or the font to get a new perspective on the text
- Commit to removing X words from each paragraph, or other mechanical methods
- Look for repetitive words and phrases, everyone has them
- Look for passive tenses and eliminate them

Working with Your Editor

You've edited the manuscript until there is no more editing in you. You've already exhausted all your friends, bought too many rounds of beer at the pub to thank your colleagues for their cryptic, usually unusable suggestions. Your partner never wants to see it again. Your grad school mentor is all mented out.

That's when you let go of it and send it to readers. And know there will still be holes to let the light in. It won't be perfect. Ever. But it will be good. If it's a journal article, editorial saturation is the time to submit it. Those peer reviewers, for all their flaws, will often have a perspective on your work that will help you rethink the parts that don't work. If you're on good terms with the journal editor from your networking, she might give it a first pass and make suggestions even before she sends it for review. Why would she waste the reviewer resources if she knows it needs more work?

A book might require a lot more feedback. It's long, it's complicated, it can't be absorbed by any reader in a single setting. This is where your acquiring editor comes in. She's your gatekeeper to accept the book, your advocate within the publishing house, your boss. Now is when she earns her keep. It's up to her to help you finish your book and do it well. You should be on good speaking terms at this point. After all, you two negotiated the outline, discussed the reviewers, jointly revised your proposal, and haggled over contract terms together.

Now she gets to help you finish the book. She's your psychologist, your cheerleader, your mentor, your favorite student, your stern judge. The strategies for starting and keeping moving forward mentioned above, while effective, often take a workout partner to implement. Another role for your editor.

You can try out ideas on restructuring. Send her passages for feedback. Ask if the tone is right. Call to talk about problems with your partner or whether you should take a sabbatical next year (duh, YES!). And it's her job to walk you through all this, professional and personal, because, as an academic, they are usually the same. If your editor is good, you'll get refocused, reenergized, and excited about the project again.

Sounds pretty miraculous? Sometimes it is. But not always. Cracks can appear. Sometimes you'll discover only then that the editor doesn't really understand your work, nor your field. (Well, she was a French lit major, after all. You just realized this?) Sometimes her suggestions won't resonate. And sometimes she might not be very responsive, even if your care and feeding is part of her job.

Why a lack of response? Just as you have teaching and service and papers and a home life, so does your editor. She's likely trying to deliver 25 books to production that year, signing another 25 for next year, and advising on the marketing of the 25 published last year. That's 74 other authors with needs, just like you have. And another 75 who are calling her and asking about future possibilities or past projects that she handled. Her equivalent of professional service? Meetings. Budgets. Training younger colleagues. If she's gonna read your stuff, it will be on a couple of slow Sunday mornings.

So pick your spots. Pick them carefully. It really can't be a partnership where your editor sits by your side helping you craft each sentence over a pot of coffee. More likely, it's a chunk of manuscript you send with some specific questions that you want the editor to address. If she can refocus you, that might be worth much more than a detailed read of every sentence.

I tell people that I haven't been caught up on my reading since 1976, when I got into publishing. Unfortunately, it's true.

The editor's other role is to manage the peer review process. In some presses, the review process is a formal one, akin to peer review on journal articles. But not always. Very often, reviewers are asked to make suggestions that will make the manuscript better, not to be the judge of its ultimate quality. As with a journal article, you can help this process. Suggest appropriate reviewers, people whose advice you would most value. Suggest to your editor what questions you'd like the reviewers to answer (she will have her own set of questions). Ask her to guide you through the reviews as to what is important and what is not. Negotiate revisions with your editor, as you would with a journal editor. The relationship you have built with your sponsoring editor should pay its dividends here, as her advice, and the advice she is able to secure from reviewers, will help you produce a better book.

Ten Tips for the Academic Writer

Besides bad eyes, reading people's manuscripts over the decades has led me to some key principles that I think can help you become a more effective academic writer. Most are stolen from people who really do know how to write. I will cite whom I stole them from as we go along.

1. Find a Hook

All those writer workshops where they train the future and has-been literati will start here. Readers start at the beginning and, if they find it compelling, move on. But what they find at the beginning needs to be compelling.

Table 7.2: Mitch's Rules for the Academic Writer

- ► 1. Find a hook
- ► 2. Tell a story
- ► 3. Include yourself
- ► 4. Write in English (or Spanish or Navajo)
- ► 5. Talk to a single reader
- ► 6. Names are important
- ► 7. Determine the detail you need
- ► 8. Present data visually
- ► 9. Make sure you can be found
- ► 10. Always think audience

Let's take, for example, the late Bud Goodall's autoethnography, *A Need to Know*. It is the story of him having to wash away everything he knew about his childhood and rethink his youth based upon the discovery in his father's bequeathal that made it clear that his dad worked for the CIA during the height of the cold war. But they were only clues and his body of evidence of this new scenario grows as the book develops. Here's how he starts it:

> My father died, either in Virginia or Maryland, at the age of 53, on the night of March 12, 1976. My mother told me that he died at home in his bed in Hagerstown, Maryland, but the Social Security Death Index indicates that he was pronounced dead in Virginia, although it doesn't say where in Virginia.
>
> I had doubts, even then, that he died at home. (Goodall 2006, p. 13)

Agatha Christie couldn't have started her mysteries any better than this. You want to read on and find out the solution to this mystery, don't you? He has you hooked.

University of South Florida education professor Valerie Janesick has written two qualitative methods books for me. In one, she uses the metaphor of dance as her way of framing qualitative concepts, stretching exercises she calls them. In the other, she uses the metaphor of Zen Buddhism, contemplative qual inquiry. These are also creative ways to get your attention and keep your interest.

2. Tell a Story

With one hand, she holds tightly to the support bar along the wall of the bathroom. I take her other hand gently in mine, wash each finger, noting the smoothness of her skin, the beauty of her long, slender fingers. "My fingernails," she says, "they're dirty." Without speaking, I run my index nail, covered with a washcloth, under each of her nails, systematically snapping out the dirt as I go. It's a good sign that she cares. Until now, she hasn't been that concerned even about urinating in bed.

When I push hard on the soap dispenser, small globs of thick, pink, liquid soap, smelling of perfumed bleach, drop onto the translucent washcloth. I load the white cloth with many squirts, hoping to wash away the lingering smell of feces, urine, perspiration, bile bags, plastic tubes, stale hair oils, and hospital odors.

She extends her arm and I slowly wash from wrist to shoulder, observing the intrusion of the spreading black bruises marking needle points. Her washed hand holds onto my wrist for support now as I unclasp her other hand from the railing. I repeat the process on that side.

"I'm going again," she says, sucking in slowly through open lips and closed teeth, eyebrows raised as though she is asking my permission and apologizing at the same time. I'm glad she is sitting on the toilet. It'll be less of a mess than before.

Carolyn Ellis's (2009, pp. 166–167) autoethnographic short story, *Maternal Connections,* tells about her reversing roles with her aged and declining mother. While it is written as a story, the paragraphs above tell you everything you need to know about the lived experience of aging, about caregivers, about the environment of the hospital, about the reversing of roles. About love. Note how she tells by showing. The details give you the big picture without Carolyn ever having to say, "Elderly people feel ashamed when they can no longer control their bowels."

Even if you don't have Carolyn's storytelling skill (few of us do) and want to stick closer to your data than Carolyn is willing to risk, telling a good story is as much of the battle as including your research and findings. There are plenty of places to learn how to write a good story. Few of them are likely to be found in a department of nursing or school of education. But being evocative, descriptive, *showing* instead of *telling* makes your qualitative writing excel.

Take the two photos below, for example. You can just say "Sydney Opera House" to describe both of them. Or you can describe the shapes, patterns, materials, and angles of the closeup view of one wall

of the building and describe it without ever naming the building.

Aristotle can be thanked for developing the principles of writing a beginning, a middle, and an end a couple of thousand years ago when people ran around in togas. The principles still apply today. Bud Goodall (2008, p. 27) outlined them as follows:

> *Conflict*: Conflict is the basis for most good stories, whether the conflict begins in a mystery to be engaged or a problem to be solved;
>
> *Connection*: The writer *creates reader identification* with the subject matter, standpoint, and style of telling the story;
>
> *Continuing Curiosity*: The writer uses the *novelty or uniqueness* in the events depicted, the characters described, the form of the story, and the truth/discovery/conclusion that is ultimately revealed to maintain reader curiosity and page-turning interest throughout the narrative; and
>
> *Climactic Satisfaction*: The ending delivers on the promise of the beginning. It's *unforgettable*. After reading the story, it stays with you.

3. Include Yourself

There's nothing wrong with you being a character in your writing, especially in qualitative research. If you've read anything since you started grad school, it's that qualitative research should be engaged and personal. "Gutsy and spirited" is what Maria Mayan (2012) calls qualitative researchers. Get into the fray, rather than hiding behind pseudo-scientific distance. There is also nothing wrong with including your reader (named "you") as a character, especially if you're providing practical advice. Even if you're using the third person, forget about using the passive voice. No one wants to read your passive, defensive voice, even if you think it sounds more scholarly. If you want readers, as well as citations, get personal.

4. Write in English (or Spanish or Navajo)

I'm tempted to put in some example (drawn from a recent Left Coast book) of abstruse, convoluted, academic language as an example of what not to do. But, fearful that one of the authors I've worked with will actually read this and recognize the passage as coming from his or her own work, I'll forego that opportunity.

You've all read stuff like that. Paragraphs, sometimes whole books, where the intent seems to be to be as obscurantist as possible, to make the reading as difficult for the reader as the writer can. Jargon. Endless paragraphs. Sentences that even your high school English teacher would be unable to diagram. References to stuff that the author knows no one else ever has (or would want to) read.

Writing is communicating. So communicate. Make it readable. Make it pleasurable. Make it intelligible to your audience. Use plain language whenever it can substitute for technical verbiage. Try to communicate more than you try to impress. Your worth as a scholar is not dependent on how many syllables are contained in your neologisms.

Your readers will appreciate it.

5. Talk to a Single Reader

She's in the room. There, by the book case or behind the pile of unread student assignments. As you stare at the blank screen, you

can feel her lurking over your shoulder. Looking. Thinking. Judging. Dr. Worst Nightmare Critic is there with you whenever you begin to write. She is as old as your university library, was critiquing articles for *Social Forces* when Strauss and Glaser were mere whelps. She has a thin mouth, always slightly downturned. When crossed, she thunders. When you timidly hand her your latest paper, the downturned mouth drops a hint lower.

She's always there when you're writing, looking over your shoulder with the slightest of disappointed sighs. But, that is enough. When you excitedly type "While homeless, the residents below the 48th Street Bridge created a support system as complex and deep as any suburban PTA," you add a prefix: "Based upon the data analyzed to date, it might be possible to hypothesize that..." Any further out on the limb, and Dr. WNC's sighs will turn to peals of derisive laughter before she rips your argument to shreds.

Qualitative researchers, like everyone else in academia, suffer the barbs of Professor Worst Nightmare Critic. In defending your work against any possible attacks from Dr. WNC, you write defensively, conservatively, passively. When you want to inhale the enthusiasm for what your colleagues have discovered in the field, you find them droning in monotone. When you want to be challenged by ideas that rock the conventional wisdom, you find them couched inside convoluted language and impenetrable jargon.

What if, instead, you were to write that article for your favorite brilliant undergraduate, the one who sits in the front row and smiles at all your jokes, whose jaw drops at the brilliant paradox with which you end your lecture and carries the conversation to office hours that follow? What if it were he looking over your shoulder while you wrote, waiting anxiously for you to pound out each sentence so he could ask a dozen breathless questions about your argument?

Wouldn't you rather read that journal article?

So take a photo of your ideal reader—the real student in your Tuesday seminar named Jason, not a hypothetical reader—and paste it on the corner of your screen. Talk directly to him; think about how excited he'll be to read your words. Dr. WNC will not like your work no matter how defensively you write it. But there are plenty of people who do want to read it. Write for them instead.

6. Names Are Important

When you see someone citing grounded theory in an article, isn't it always followed by "(Glaser and Strauss 1967)"? Or member check by "(Lincoln and Guba 1986)"? Grand tour questions by "(Spradley 1979)"? Capture the name of a technique, a setting, a concept, write about it, and popularize it, and the world will have to cite you forevermore. Not bad for your citation count, but it also gives you a calling card for your career. So think carefully about what you call what you do, where you are doing it, or the theory you have developed. Market it by using that term in all your publications and conference talks. Convince your friends to use the same term. They may not even use it the same way that you do. But a good name will get both you and your ideas out into the world. Right now, we're working on books on contemplative qualitative inquiry and diffractive ethnography. I'm hoping both terms catch on, because we'll have books with those titles.[1] I've had these battles before. When Egon Guba and Yvonna Lincoln invented *Fourth Generation Evaluation* (that term gets tossed around a lot), they described a continual collaborative process of testing out ideas with various groups of stakeholders. I couldn't get them to change to a better term than "hermeneutic dialectics," which has disappeared beneath the waves.

Even if it isn't a brand new concept, try it out. Ask any old scholar about mixed methods, and he'll tell you that term is not much different than the term triangulation used 40 year ago. But it was dusted off by John Creswell and others and now has its own research tradition, society, journal, and conference. The power of intellectual branding and marketing can't be overestimated.

7. Use No More Detail Than Necessary

> The critical task in qualitative research is not to accumulate all the data you can but to "can" (get rid of) most of the data you accumulate. (Wolcott 2009, p. 35)

The more I read his work, the more I think that the late educational anthropologist Harry Wolcott was a Zen master. Write your first draft before you do your research! Can as much of your data as you can! But he's right. By the time you get to writing articles or books, you will be awash in data: interview transcripts, field notes, photos, drawings, code books. The key, according to Harry, is to find the right way to get rid of most of it, so you can tell an effective story. After all, what you want to produce from your research is that story that captivates the reader [tip #2]. When they're hooked [tip #1], they can ask you for more. But you need to get them hooked first.

This should be easier if you take my advice in chapter 2 seriously. Turn your research project into a variety of products for a number of audiences. If each is a well-crafted narrative, you will have plenty of original data to back each up without bogging down the reader in too much prose.

8. Present
Data Visually

If you wanted to discuss rule making

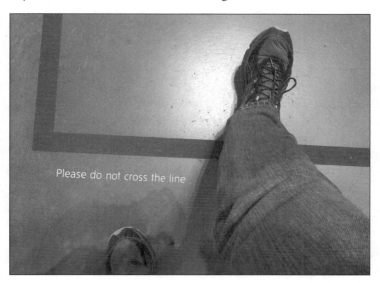

or rule breaking
or technological

change,

there are ways other than using text. Need I say more?

9. Make Sure You Can Be Found

We addressed this earlier in the book, but it bears repeating. We live in an era where there is a never-ending barrage of information being flung at each of us daily. How are people going to find you and your work in all the din?

Part of the answer is to be proactive, to market your own work (see chapter 9). Postings on listservs and other specialized groups, social media, using your publisher's and your university's public relations mechanisms, sending samples to key people.

The other important element to consider is optimizing the chance of being discovered by someone looking for material on your topic. What do search engines use to find information on a subject? Well, your title, your abstract, the keywords you provide, as we discussed in chapter 2. The table of contents of your book. Spending time focusing on those, rather than dashing them off at the end is well worth your time. Whatever terms you hope people will use to find you should be prominently situated in your metadata.

10. Always Think Audience

Audience—the most important word for the published writer. Is anyone reading your ideas? If you're writing for yourself, you didn't really need this book and should send it back for a refund. Then check out how to self-publish through Amazon or Lulu. But if you're hoping to influence your colleagues, your students, your local politicians, your local community, your focus should be on your audience.

Who is your audience? Sigh. If you don't know that by now, go back to page 1 of this book and start reading all over again. A bit more carefully this time.

But if you do know, put down this book (you can always look at the last couple of chapters later), paste Jason's picture on your computer screen, shut off your email, and get working on telling him all the great stuff you've learned in your latest study.

Chapter 8

Understanding Publishing Contracts

The traditional model of commercial publishing is based on contractual agreements between the author, creator of the material, and the publisher, who produces and distributes it. These agreements, for all their legal mumbo-jumbo, rarely vary from a single fixed point: if a commercial organization is going to invest substantial money in the production, distribution, and marketing of a writer's work, they believe they have the right to maximize their income from that effort. Thus, publishing contracts will include absolutist clauses like:

> Author hereby grants to the Publisher the sole and exclusive right to print, produce, publish and sell in all languages the Work or any abridgement of the Work or any part of the Work in serial or volume form, hardback, paperback or electronic Versions or in any other format for the legal term of copyright throughout the World, and the right to authorize others to do so.

> [These formats can include] dramatization or documentary (including by stage, film, radio, television, internet or by any other medium whatsoever), merchandising (including by the manufacture, licensing, sale or hire of goods and services or by any other means whatsoever), audio or audiovisual recording (including by film, record, tape, Compact Disc, DVD, MP3 or by

Essentials of Publishing Qualitative Research by Mitchell Allen.
111–120. © 2016 Left Coast Press, Inc. All rights reserved.

means of any contrivance whatsoever whether now in existence or hereafter invented)...

They can turn your work into a children's cartoon and its author into a bobblehead doll if they wish. Solely and exclusively.

Authors have railed against losing rights to their intellectual children for as long as publishing has existed, with only sporadic success. Successful trade book authors with aggressive agents are often able to auction off individual rights to an intellectual property (hardback rights, paperback rights, film rights, audio rights, the plush toy) to the highest bidder. For example, the best-selling trilogy of novels, *Fifty Shades of Grey*, initially published in the UK, had regional hardcover and paperback rights sold in the United States, translation rights in almost 40 languages, eBook, audio book, and movie rights (www.eljamesauthor.com/), not to mention the Fifty Shades of Grey Official Pleasure Collection (www.thewrap.com/fifty-shades-sex-toy-sales-please-universal-even-unlicensed/). But for every E. L. James, there are tens of thousands of less successful authors who, because of the overwhelming differential between supply and demand, accept these draconian terms. This is invariably true in academic publishing. The profit margin is slim and the possibility of subsidiary rights sale so slight that there is little room for authorial bargaining.

This is the devil's bargain. If you want to be published in the A-level journals or in a book from a 400-year-old university press, you gotta give up your rights to them. And you have to do what the publisher tells you to do. To fail usually means torture by Vegemite or Velveeta, depending on your geographical location. The bargaining power you have is usually small, but there are a couple of things you should look for when the contract to sign pops up in your inbox.

Contracts for Journal Articles

This contract usually arrives after the journal editor has accepted your article and turned your final manuscript over to her production department. For article agreements, there is a minimum of leeway. After all, your article is being published in connection with many other articles in a fixed time frame. Dealing with dozens, maybe hundreds of authors, the publisher doesn't want to separately negotiate each and every contract. The process would grind to a halt. Special requests generally won't be accommodated; it's almost always take it or leave it. What should be particularly important to you are two things:

1) What rights do I have to my own material if I publish the article with you? It is common practice that authors can reuse their own material in future articles and books that they write. But not always. If you're in doubt as to whether the publisher allows this, get it in writing. But what else can you do with the various pieces of your article? Do you have the right to send offprints to various colleagues? Hand out the chapter to your students or in your workshop? Grant the right to others to use the figures you created for this paper? Post some or all of the article on your website? Give it to your university repository? Do you have any say in who the publisher allows to reprint the piece? Each publisher has different policies on the uses of your material. Many publishers will include this information in the contract. Others will post their definition of authors' rights on their websites or in their instructions to you. You need to ask now, before you sign the contract. If it is too restrictive, ask questions. But don't just say, "This is too restrictive." Be specific: "I run regular seminars on how to do focus groups and want to hand out my article to the attendees. Is that permitted?" If they agree, get it in writing.

2) How much am I involved in the production of my article? Will I get to see proofs of it? Can I make corrections? What is required of me in terms of providing appropriate images, copyright permission (see more on these below)? This also might not be in the contract, but you need to know the parameters of your level of control before you say yes. Afterwards, they can just ignore you. Either the journal's editor or, more likely, the managing editor of the journal, who often works for the publisher, should be able to answer these questions and describe their normal production procedures.

If the answers are not satisfactory, you might try to negotiate better terms, but because of the assembly-line nature of journal production, you should be prepared to pull back the article and look for another home for it. Of course, if you have been diligent about the research process before submitting the article, you would likely know the answers to these questions already and won't have to face this dilemma.

Some smaller or more informal journals don't have a formal contracting process. This can be dangerous as well, as your rights might not be protected. While you don't have to hire a lawyer to invent your own contract, it would be good to lay out in writing the journal's rights and your rights to the article. Write up the topics that concern you—reviewing the manuscript, reusing the material, controlling further rights—and send it to the journal editor for a signature or at least an email accepting those terms. In one case I've recently dealt with, the lack of a written agreement between contributors and journal prevented us from being able to reprint the theme issue of the journal in book form.

Book Contracts

Book contracts are more often singular arrangements. This usually gives you more leeway to negotiate with the publisher, at least in some areas. If you don't like the publisher's warranties, holding you responsible for not plagiarizing, libeling your dean, or fomenting insurrection, you're out of luck. Those clauses are written by lawyers and are not likely to be amended. Similarly, publishers have clear economic models, publication procedures, and marketing strategies for their books. They have dealt with enough situations to know not to be specific about some of their promises to you. Getting your publisher to put the price or the publication date of your book in writing is unlikely. Nor will you have final say over the title, the production processes, or the final pages that go to the printer. The publisher does. But there are some places where you can use your knowledge of publishing and your negotiating skills to help your cause.

Title

Book contracts will have a book title on them prefaced with "tentatively entitled." The finalization of the title generally won't occur until the point where the book starts being advertised. An accommodating press will actively involve the author in the final selection of the title. But not all publishers will. If your book has to have a certain title, now is the time to resolve that. Ask them to delete the "tentatively entitled" from the contract if you know what title you need. Better to have that battle now, and not sign the contract if you can't get your way, than to have the title "wrong" throughout the book's history. But publishers are as concerned with signaling your audience as you are. They may come up with a better title than you. So only fight this battle if you really feel the publisher's suggestions are off base.

Delivery Date

The easiest item to negotiate is the due date for the manuscript. While a publisher might give you a due date (I usually ask the author to provide his or her own), we've all heard the litany of excuses for late manuscripts. Almost as many grandmothers (beloved aunts, cherished neighbors) die within a few weeks of a book due date as do students' adored relatives during finals week. Ditto computer crashes. My favorite is the author who was kept from working on her book because she had to "put a llama down." The publisher wants an *accurate* delivery date even more than you do. Having negotiated the date, plan on meeting it. And keep the publisher apprised as to your progress or lack of progress.

Page Length

Page length and number of illustrations are inherently unknown before you start writing. Some modification in those areas is not uncommon. Chapter 6 has more information on how to estimate your book's length as part of your book proposal. This would be a good time to find out the publisher's parameters on length and leave yourself as much flexibility as you can in the contract.

Illustrations

This used to be a big issue before the days of digital publishing. Illustrations were costly to the publisher because they required special production and printing processes to accommodate them. That's no longer an issue, and most publishers are welcoming of black and white illustrations for books. Your contract could specify a maximum number of illustrations allowed. Make sure it fits your needs. Also remember that a picture is worth 1,000 words (actually 425 words, the number of words that a full page illustration would replace in an average Left Coast book page). The more illustrations, the fewer words you are likely to be allowed.

Color illustrations are still an issue; color printing is done on a different kind of printing press with different paper and ink and is substantially more expensive. Make sure the publisher will accommodate your desire for color illustrations if you need them.

Editions

Will the publisher produce a paperback? An eBook? Those items will sometimes be in the contract and sometimes not. If not, you can often negotiate a promise for them and a timing for when they will be released. Get that commitment in writing, whether in the contract or in an email from your editor. The publisher will likely have a general strategy for sequencing various book editions, but they do often make exceptions. This is one area in which you should know your publisher's intentions and can push for concessions.

Royalties

Royalties are the first place most people will look to negotiate. Royalties will vary by author, type of book, and publisher. Royalties are calculated in two different ways, and you need to know on which one your payments are based. Publishers will only use one of these systems in calculating royalties on all their books, so asking them to use the other for your particular book is a non-starter.

- Payment on "list price" or "gross sales" is common in trade publishing. You sell 100 books, the publisher lists the price at $30. You are owed a percentage of $3,000 ($30 x 100) in sales. In trade publishing, the publisher often has to give high discounts to bookstores to sell books. Trade authors had no control over the discounts given away by the publisher's sales department, so they and their agents have learned to ask for royalties to be based on the list price.
- Payment on "cash received" or "net sales" is the basis of almost all royalty calculations on academic books. The publisher received $2,258 for the 100 copies of your book they sold. Some were sold at full price off their website, some at 40 percent discount through Amazon, some at 25 percent discount to libraries, some at 30 percent at a conference, and so forth. You get paid based on the amount the publisher actually collected from purchasers.

In academic works, royalties can range from 0 percent for an edited volume, monograph, or a revised dissertation to 15 percent of net sales for a book by a well-known author or for a high profile title that the publisher wants badly. Textbooks usually range from 10 to 20 percent because of their higher sales potential. But if royalties are a percentage of sales, you can have a high royalty percentage and still make very little money if the publisher doesn't sell many copies. Your initial research of publishers will give you some idea how aggressive they are in selling their titles.

An intermediate strategy that often works is to ask for a sliding scale. If you sell more than XX books (500, 1,000, 2,000), the royalty percentage increases. Each publisher has a breakeven point, where the book is clearly making them a profit. They can afford to be more generous with you once they're in the black. Why isn't every publications contract written like that? Because a majority of books don't reach that point. The publisher, not you, has to swallow the losses if they don't. They will offer the sliding scale on books that they believe have a strong upside, ones that could go viral. But on your everyday edited collection, you are likely to meet with resistance from what might feel to you to be a reasonable request.

Advances and Grants

An advance against royalties is just that: the publisher pays you money that you will ultimately earn in royalties in advance of the publication of the book, before you have earned those royalties. This is common in trade publishing where the authors are professional writers and live off advances and royalties while they are writing. Most academics live off their university salaries, not their book royalties, and don't write books that can sell tens of thousands of copies that generate salary-sized royalties. So most academic book publishers don't offer advances. Even if they do, those advances need to get paid off. You won't see another penny from your publisher until the amount earned in royalties exceeds the amount of the advance you were paid.

In some cases, though, advances can be negotiated. The most common advance is for the index (see chapter 9). You may also be able to negotiate an advance for unusual expenses that you the author might incur while preparing the book. If your book is reprinting images or articles from copyrighted sources, and those come with permission fees, the publisher will sometimes give you an advance for those. You need to hire someone to draw maps or charts for you or run some computer models. It's worth asking for an advance on those so you're not out of pocket.

If your publisher really wants the book badly and thinks they will do very well with it, they might offer you a grant rather than an advance, meaning that the publisher is covering those costs and not taking them out of your royalties. Either way, you need to pay careful attention to the amount of the advance or the grant. If the publisher agrees to $1,500 and it turns out that the permissions or illustrations you require cost $5,000, guess who has to pick up the rest? Know what those costs will be before you ask for the advance or grant.

If your unusual expenses include a trip to Paris to check that obscure archive one more time, I would recommend not asking the publisher to pay for it.

Marketing

Publishers have standard ways of marketing your book. They won't put the details in the contract other than to say they have the right to market as they wish. If there are specific things your book needs, now is the time to address them. It is unlikely they will end up in the contract—publishers tend to be shy about that level of legal commitment to specific marketing tasks—but you can and should get a written outline of what the publisher intends to do for your book before you sign on the dotted line. Ask your editor for it.

Right of First Refusal

This clause states that you have to offer the publisher your next book as well as this one. This is another holdover from trade publishing. If you're writing for a living and Random House turns you into a bestselling author, they will (often rightly) claim credit for that and expect that they will get to publish your next book. In academic publishing, your reputation comes off of many more things than just the books you publish. If the publisher has this clause in your contract, I suggest that you insist that it be removed. Your next book might not be in an area that this publisher handles well. If you lose that battle—and you shouldn't—then try a backup strategy. When the time for your next book comes, offer that publisher a volume of your poetry written on a cruise around the Caribbean last summer. Write a couple of sample pieces to show that you mean it. When they turn that down, you can take your more academic book proposal to another press and still meet the letter of the agreement you signed.

Copyright

This is one that gets many authors up in arms, but isn't as big a deal as you think. You want the copyright for the long term, so that you can reprint, reuse, redo this work down the road. But the contract has the book copyrighted in the name of the publisher. If so, there should also be a clause offering the copyright back to you if the book goes out of print. That won't help much. With the availability of printing on demand, your book could stay in print forever.

But the copyright isn't really what you should be focused on. Look instead at that clause that gives the publisher all the *publishing rights* to your book, the "sole and exclusive rights" mentioned above. It doesn't matter whether or not you have the copyright, if you've signed away those rights, the publisher can do pretty much anything they want to with your intellectual property (including creating the bobblehead doll) until they take it out of print.

The copyright notice on page 4 of the book signals to outsiders where to ask for permission to use your material. And, because you've signed away all those publishing rights, you can't grant that permission anyway; you have to send those requests to the publisher. You've made it harder for those outsiders to ask for permission—they have to find you, and you're more likely to be changing addresses than the publisher is. If they finally find you, you can only tell them to ask someone else, your publisher. So focus on that: If you need to control specific publishing rights to the book—if, for example, you have a documentary in the works or a friend is creating your bobblehead—ask for those. And, if you demand the copyright, it might be possible to obtain it; though most publishers would prefer to keep it for the reasons stated here.

There are other things you might find important and want included in the contract. Ask about them. Members of the Author's Guild have access to their model contract, written with the needs of the author, rather than the publisher, in mind. Many of those clauses would not be appropriate for scholarly books, but it might be worth the investment to join the Guild for their contract guidelines.

Authors are often hesitant to make requests of the publisher. What if the publisher decides to withdraw the contract because the author has made too many demands? That should not be too serious a concern. By the time the publisher has offered a contract, they are committed to publishing the book. The wrangling over contract terms is one of the details in that process. True, there are cases when your non-negotiable demands could result in withdrawal of a contract. More likely, you will be able to work out some of the specific concerns you have during this process. Even the requests the publisher cannot agree with should warrant an explanation as to why. And, if you have effectively submitted the book to multiple presses and have more than one contract offer, you might be able to get the most favorable terms of all.

Chapter 9

The Production Process

- *It took two years to come out, and even then they printed the map upside down.*
- *There were so many typos in the article that I was embarrassed to include it in my tenure packet.*
- *I didn't realize all the work that was expected of me to produce a camera-ready book. I never would have done it if I knew.*

These horror stories are all too common. They reinforce the traditional ambivalence scholars feel toward publishers. Journal editors and book publishers aren't really bottom-feeding scumbags. They want your work to look good, want many people to read it, want it to come out in a timely fashion, just as you do. But their concerns are not only with your piece, but with the many other articles and books that are also running through their pipeline. So they develop systems for getting things done. Timelines for doing them. Queues to maximize the efficiency with which all these steps are completed. To the extent that you can make your efforts fit theirs, the process of getting published will be quicker, easier, less painful. But each publisher recognizes that academic writers have their own identities and needs. Often the press will circumvent their own processes to accommodate you, but not always, particularly if it interferes with the functioning of their overall systems. The more you know about how those systems work, which points are negotiable and which are not, the more likely you are to have your special requests accommodated. If that sounds like more research—research on the publication process this time—that's just what it is. This chapter is designed, then, to give you the basics of that process so that you can formulate good questions to your journal editor or publisher about what is fixed and what can be modified to maximize the chances that your piece will turn out the way you want it to. While there are differences between these processes in journal publishing and book publishing, much of what occurs is the same. So we'll consider the two together.

Your job doesn't end when you've turned in the manuscript. Publishers will need your attention during production of a journal article or your book. Try to be quick, responsive, and cooperative. That helps speed the process along. The more complex it gets, the longer it takes, the more likely there will be an error in the final product. While there is a rumor deeply held in academia that your publisher is supposed to make your work perfect—and we do try—error is part of the human condition. So is the annoyance factor. A journal editor or acquisitions editor who had endless fights with an author throughout production may just decide it isn't worth those battles again the next time you submit something, no matter how good your work is.

Journal Articles

Once you have an acceptance in hand from the journal editor, you will usually be asked for other things as well. Follow orders, as hard as that is for most academics. Most journals run like automotive assembly lines. They have a flow of articles, each of which requires a bunch of steps to prepare for publication. The author who insists his text be printed in a different font than the journal's standard one slows down the process, not only for his article but for the ones before and after. And you won't get what you want anyway. This is not the time to innovate, but to follow instructions.

Journal style. You will be asked to follow the journal's style guide. That guide should be on their website or should be one of the standard style guides used in scholarly publishing (MLA, APA, CMS, for example).

Journals pride themselves on consistency, including consistency of the style they use. If you mess around too much with the style guidelines, they'll just send your manuscript back to you and ask you to redo it.

Ancillary materials. You will be asked to provide some ancillary material. Make sure you provide those. They all represent parts of the machine that needs to be installed with your article before it can be published. These items might include:

- Your full contact information
- A contract, giving the journal the right to publish your intellectual property
- A biographical sketch of a specified length
- Figures or photos in camera-ready format (see below)
- Permissions required on copyrighted material used in your article (see below)
- A statement assuring the reader there is no conflict of interests in your work, and sometimes a statement of the funding source for your research

The journal editor or managing editor, if the journal has one, can usually answer any questions you have about these items.

Schedule. Ask for a schedule for production and what tasks will be required of you. What issue is the article likely to appear in? Will you be reading proofs of your typeset and edited article and, if so, approximately when. How much time will you have to respond? As above, this is not the time to try to change the system. If you can't meet their schedules, or have any specific issues concerning your article, let them know in advance so they can reschedule the publication date.

Title, abstract, keywords. Before submitting the final manuscript, take one more look at your title, abstract, and keywords. Now is the time to get them right. They are the ways in which people find your work. Make sure that everyone who will want to read you is included.

When questions come from the managing editor and the copyeditor, and when you receive proofs to read, respond expeditiously. You are part of a journal issue with a bunch of other authors. The issue doesn't get published until everyone's material is complete. Be considerate. Everyone else wants their pieces published quickly, too.

Illustrations and Copyright Permissions

The items that seem to bedevil academic authors the most, for both books and journals, are providing usable illustrations and correct copyright permissions. Most journals and publishers will have explicit guidelines on their website or that can be sent to you by the editor. Read them; that's why they're there.

Illustrations. Once upon a time, you would send your prints, slides, or negatives to the publisher, and they would convert them for print. With the digitization of visual images, this has become a moving target that changes regularly with changes in technology. If illustrations are to be included in your article or book, it should have been discussed in advance with the editor. A few issues reoccur regularly:

- The fact that the image looks good on a computer screen doesn't mean it is good enough resolution for a printed journal issue. There are different printer formulas for photographs and **line art** (maps, charts, flow charts, diagrams) contained in the publisher's instructions. If you're uncertain whether your images meet the requirements, send the illustrations in early and ask the editor to tell you whether they're good enough. If they are not, she should be able to give you instructions on how to make them better. If you're trying to use a digital photo and the original is low resolution—and most images pulled from the web are—you might have to accept that you can't use it.

- There is still a huge cost differential between printing black and white and color illustrations. Don't assume that your illustrations will appear in color. Check with the journal editor first. Journals that regularly accept color images are pretty easy to identify in a brief skim of recent issues. If they must be printed in black and white, you can check how your images will appear by converting them to grayscale in Photoshop or some similar program.

- Don't embed your illustrations in the manuscript. Leave a spot in the text for each one with the legend "FIGURE 1 GOES HERE" and submit each illustration in a separate electronic file, labeling the file clearly so the proper image can be placed in the right place when the article is being typeset.

- Ask the publisher for the proper resolution, size, and format before you scan any images. If you are uncertain that you have it right, send a sample scan to the publisher to confirm before you scan the other 20.
- Figures usually require captions. A separate text file with all your captions (and the image numbers they go with) will avoid problems later on.
- Similar guidelines usually apply to tables.

Copyright permissions. If you thought getting the illustrations together was bad, they're nothing compared to copyright permissions. This is not the place to give a detailed explanation of what requires copyright permission, nor do I have the credentials in intellectual property law to do so. The specifics of what requires copyright permission revolves around the concept of **fair use** of a certain amount of copyrighted material. Interpretation of fair use varies between fields and between publishers; it is fuzzy enough that something that might be okay for one journal won't be for another. So start with your editor. If you're using quotes from a secondary source, illustrations from another source, unpublished material that is not yours, quotes from newspaper articles or other media broadcasts, poetry, drama, pretty much anything that you didn't write yourself, there might be the need to get permission from the original creator or the entity that controls its publishing rights. Here is where the journal editor or managing editor should be able to guide you. Look at the guidelines on the journal's website. If there's any uncertainty in your mind, ask.

Copyright permissions might require months of work to finalize, and your article might sit in limbo until all the copyright permissions have been secured. Don't wait until you have turned in the final manuscript to start working on these. If you want some more bad news, some copyright holders will ask you for money to pay for use of the material. Even if you are an underpaid academic or starving graduate student, these are your costs. The journal editor should be able to tell you if the cost is reasonable and if there are any strategies for trying to get the fee waived or reduced.

Submitting Your Book Manuscript

The first important hurdle here is the "acceptance" of the manuscript. Our contract, like most, says something to the effect that the manuscript has to be "in content and form satisfactory to the Publisher and ready for copyediting and production." Maybe your manuscript ran a wee bit too long. Or was delivered a few weeks (or years) later than you promised. Or you really really really need to add two more photos beyond your allotted limit. Until the publisher, usually through your editor, accepts the manuscript, you're still in limbo. If there is a peer review process at the end, or a university press board to convince, that process also could take a while.

Table 9.1: Book Manuscript Checklist

- ▶ Front matter—title page, table of contents, list of figures
- ▶ Author biography and photo
- ▶ Acknowledgments
- ▶ Consistent subheads
- ▶ Foreword by important scholar
- ▶ High resolution illustrations
- ▶ Permissions for all copyrighted material
- ▶ Finalize title
- ▶ Suggestions for cover design
- ▶ Style sheet and instructions for the copyeditor
- ▶ Listing of scheduling limitations
     and…
- ▶ The manuscript

Before you submit your manuscript, you should have received detailed instructions from the publisher as to what "ready for copyediting and production" means. There might be the narrowest details (two spaces after a period) to fairly mundane stuff (12 point Times Roman font with 1" margins on all sides) to fairly abstruse instructions that you might not fully understand. If you don't get those instructions, can't find them on the publisher's website, or are not clear on them, ask your acquiring editor. Of course, you weren't thinking about this three months ago while you were grappling with the main point you were trying to make in chapter 3, so your manuscript is probably not exactly in the requested format. Your acquiring editor should be able to tell you what they really insist upon and what can slide a bit. Rarely will they insist on everything.

Like the journal article, there are bits of flotsam and jetsam that are supposed to accompany a finished book manuscript. The publisher's guide should alert you to those various pieces. They will usually include:

Front matter. Create a title page, just so you can be sure that you and the publisher are in agreement on the book title and that they spell your name right and include the correct middle initial. Create a table of contents, then review it. It's a sales tool for the book, a way in which a potential reader can skim quickly and get a sense of how you have organized your book. Make sure your chapter titles clearly do that.

Author biography and photo. This is a requirement for most academic books. There is probably an ideal length for this that the publisher has in mind. Ask. Like the biographical sketch you provided in the book proposal, its function is to convince the reader that you know what you're talking about and are a serious scholar writing a serious book. Crib from the biography you did for the proposal. Some publishers want a photo of the author to further personalize you.

Acknowledgments. The bad news: Try to construct an Acknowledgments section of everyone who helped you with your book in a single sitting. It won't happen. You're bound to forget someone. Your 11th grade English teacher who taught you proper grammar. One of the members of your dissertation committee. The cute Tuesday barista at the local Peet's who always had a smile for you and got your writing sessions going. How could you forget him? The good news: You will have a couple of other opportunities to add more names during the copyediting and proofreading phases. Start building that list when you start writing your book. And be reasonable. When Acknowledgments gets onto its third or fourth page, people will stop reading. If you miss *anyone* after thanking the first 150 people, that person is bound to be annoyed.

Subheads. The publisher will usually want you to indicate which subhead is level 1, 2, 3. If that phrase is meaningless to you, then go look at a style guide. It's also a good opportunity for you to make sure you have included subheads and that there is a hierarchy, so a level 2 head has a level 1 head above it. Review your subheads to make sure all subheads at each level are formatted the same.

Foreword/Preface/Introduction. Which term do you use to label the first piece in the book? The **Foreword** (note the spelling, the *words before* the book starts, not Forward, the direction ahead of you) is usually written by someone other than you. Whether the book needs an external foreword and, if so, who should write it is one of the items that you discuss with your editor. The **Preface** is usually your first piece of writing, most often a personal statement on how the book came about. Both are usually brief in academic works, two to five manuscript pages. The **Introduction** is the substantive beginning of the book, where you lay out what you are trying to accomplish intellectually and how the book is structured to accomplish that.

Other Key Decisions

There are a lot of other items that get finalized at the beginning of the book production process. Address your questions to the publisher now; changes are harder—often impossible—to make later in the process.

Title. If your title is still tentative, now is the time to arm wrestle with the publisher about it. Your editor might be your direct contact here, but there are likely some editorial supervisors and marketing people who are also in on the decision. In some ways, the title decision is as important as the contents of the book. If people aren't attracted by the title to look into the book, they may never get to your wonderful prose and scintillating ideas. There is no right way to proceed here. As a publisher, I've insisted on specific book titles at times and gotten it wrong. I've let the author have their way and gotten it wrong. Sometimes I did get it right and the author was later appreciative of my choice, and vice versa. It is rare that a "compromise" title works. What is crucial is that the keywords in the title and subtitle are things that will draw the main audiences you wish to reach.

Cover design. Who doesn't want the kind of cover that you can frame and put on your office wall. But someone else who knows nothing about your book is going to design it. And the publisher is going to have the final say in what it looks like. If you want to be involved in the process, you need to take the lead. Find out when the cover is going to be designed. Often that time is before your book manuscript is completed. Your acquisitions editor should know this and should keep you in the loop. Some publishers have specific templates; some book series have them, too. If you have a specific aura you want for your cover, you need to convey that to your editor as early as you can. Fonts, colors, size of the title, all those are items that you can make suggestions about. If there is a specific image you want, make sure your editor knows where and how to get it. If it comes from a copyrighted source, make sure they are willing to pay for the permission to reuse it. That might require some work on your part—and some money if they won't pay but are willing to use it if you pay.

The best way of expressing what you want is by showing visual examples. Find some book covers you really like and send them to your editor—and be able to explain *why* you like them. Some authors try to mock up their own cover, but unless they have a design background themselves, their mock-ups are usually horrible and are easily ignored. The more information in the hands of your editor, who usually gives instructions to the design department, the more specific she can be with the designer and the more likely the product that results will match your ideal. There is no guarantee you will see the cover they design, but ask your editor (nicely) if you can have some input, and it will often happen. If what comes back is unacceptable, then you need to respond with rational, cogent reasons why. Your aesthetic sense is usually not a persuasive reason. If the book is about new media and the cover comes back with a Victorian font, that's a good reason. Give constructive suggestions; try to be helpful instead of critical. Contractually, the final decision is almost always in the hands of the publisher, so you need to be able to plead your case rather than demand change.

Editing style. If there are things you specifically want to see retained in your writing style, create a style sheet for the publisher, who should be able to pass it to the production people. You want Black, White, Indigenous capitalized? Then make it clear. You want "(re)pose" to be bracketed, put it in your style sheet. The publisher will usually instruct copyeditors to use one of the major style guides. But exceptions can be made if there are good content reasons for them. And make sure you use those words consistently in the book yourself. You should even consider including notes to the copyeditor if you want specific help from her: "Copyeditor: This sentence seems to ramble, can you help me focus it better." The more you can help the copyeditor target things that you think will help you, the better the editing is likely to be.

Production process and schedule. The publisher needs to slot your book in with all the others they are currently publishing. If you've delivered your manuscript on time and in good shape, you should get rewarded for that. If it's late and missing a bunch of pieces, it might have to sit in the queue until one of the production slots opens up. Your prepublication research should have already informed you about how a book is produced at this press and where you have input. Now is the time to confirm those details. Creating a schedule for various production people is one of the things the publisher needs to accomplish. You should make sure your needs are included in preparing this schedule. If the date of Proof to Author coincides with your sister's wedding or your long-awaited trip to Maui, point it out in advance so the publisher can adjust the schedule. Provide the publisher with your unavailability dates when you submit the manuscript, so they can build their schedule around it. Make sure you know how much time you are likely to have to review the copyediting, to read proofs, and to do the index (see below).

Before this, your acquiring editor has been your steady contact, the one who has answered your endless questions. At this point, she usually passes the baton on to the production team. As I've been suggesting throughout the book, having a good personal relationship with the decision makers is always a good idea. Find out who is going to be shepherding your book through the production process and start building those bridges. You will have lots of question about production, particularly if this is your first book, and this is the person who controls that process. If you show you're interested, cooperative, humane, you'll be included in the process more often and are more likely to affect that process.

During the Production Process

It was a royal pain, getting all those illustrations in proper form, tracking down a permission from some obscure publisher in Paris, and trying to find the name of that grad assistant from three years ago whom you needed to acknowledge in the front matter. Everything is in the publisher's hands, the book is going to be produced in a few months, and now you can relax.

Not quite. In most cases you will be asked to be involved in the production process at least a few times, and not at the times and places of your choosing. The requests from the publisher's production team will usually come unexpectedly and demand an immediate response. Just before your vacation. A week before a grant deadline. While you're dealing with a sick father. Or all the above (don't they always coincide?). If you've been talking with the production team already, you'll know more about when these requests are going to arrive and how much time you really have to answer them. Schedules usually have a bit of slack built in to accommodate the author's grant deadline and the copyeditor's sick kid. But don't assume that you can pick your preferred time to resolve the issue and to have engines start up again. Whether the production team is directly employed by the publisher or are freelancers, production teams can only survive financially by having a steady flow of work. If you hold the machine up too long, they'll move on to the next project and get back to yours only when they finish that one. Cooperation and communication between authors and production team can often result in lightning fast production (one book this season went from manuscript to the printer in less than a month); otherwise, production can drift in back eddies for what seems forever. You have some control through the relationship you build with the project manager and your responsiveness to production questions. So here are the points where you will typically be asked to be involved in the production process.

Point 1: Here's where You Screwed Up

This is typically a terse email from the project manager:

- Missing permissions on Figure 2.2.
- The photo of that homeless family under the bridge is too low resolution to print. Do you have a better quality version? (*And*

getting that photo was an act of heroism. All the way down to securing the permission to use it. Can't they just print it? So what if it's a little dark!!)

- Can you cut your biographical sketch by 50 words?

The production people will want all the little bits that you forgot despite your best efforts. They have not created hurdles for you just to make you squirm, but because those pieces are impediments to a quick, smooth, error-free production process. So chase down the permission, see if you have a better version of that photo, and so forth. In some presses, the book will stay in limbo until the last piece is in. Other publishers will go forward with a few loose ends still unresolved. It's worth a call to your project manager to ask what kind of timetable is needed and the consequences if certain missing pieces take longer.

Point 2: Review the Copyediting

Copyediting at most scholarly presses is light. If you had rough passages in the text, they're likely to still be there. It's most often a mechanical rather than artistic process—grammar correct, punctuation appropriate, completeness of references—all formatted to the style guide the press uses and design codes inserted for the typesetter to follow. At this point, your job is to review what the copyeditor did to ensure she did not do violence to your intent. If the copyeditor was competent, which is usually the case (though not always), she will have cleaned up a lot of technical things that you missed and maybe polished a line or two that needed it. This is also your last chance to rewrite a bad sentence, replace an awkward phrase with a better one, add a reference to a key new article. Occasionally, an author will feel this is a chance to rewrite his or her manuscript, which was completed in a hurry. Resist the temptation. If the text is significantly revised from the original submission, your changes might be overruled by the project manager. After all, a new draft of your manuscript would require copyediting all over again.

If you have issues with changes the copyeditor made, start first by expressing your concerns to the copyeditor (or the project manager, whichever sent you the copyedited manuscript to review). Be nice about it and focus on the things that you think are most important to fix. If you feel like you're being stonewalled, then go to your acquiring editor for help. Generally, things can get worked out. But I've heard from a few authors incensed about how the copyeditor "destroyed" their manuscript. Rarely was that true. Even more rarely was the copyediting redone or ignored in favor of the author's approach.

Point 3: Page Proofs

This is your last chance to catch anything stupid. With the advent of electronic production systems, most of what you see in these pages is close to what you submitted and reviewed in the copyediting. You will still find problems: typos that you and the copyeditor both missed. An incorrect reference. You will also find a sentence you wish you had expressed better. Such re-writes are usually not possible at this point; that was why you were sent the copyedited manuscript to review. But if there is something that absolutely must change, make a case for it with the project manager. This is one place where a good relationship might get you more than otherwise. Occasionally, the designer will forget a photo or place one upside down. Make sure you have the right captions attached to the right photos. You are no longer seeing the text clearly, you've looked at it too many times. So buy a good friend a bottle of wine (to drink *after* reviewing the proofs) and go through the proofs with someone else's fresh eyes as well as your own. There usually will be strong admonitions from the project manager not to change anything, just correct typos. The publisher will have a professional proofreader simultaneously reviewing the text, but for other things: running head consistency, correctness of the front matter, fonts that amazingly switched size in midsentence. Don't forget to look for *big* things. Did they spell your name right on the title page and is the book title correct? Did they include all of the chapters? Include all the illustrations? We just published a book where the running head at the top of each page misspelled the title of the book. It went past a whole raft of people, including the author.

Point 4: Index

Indexing is the bane of a book author's existence. It has to be done at the end of the production process when you're sick of the whole thing. It's a lot of work. It's hard work. There are a minimum of shortcuts you can take. And the time frame is usually compressed. Everyone wants the book out and this is the last step.

To index the book is to reconceptualize it for the convenience of the unknown reader who is looking for something specific in your book, not necessarily what you are trying to present. If your book is an ethnography of public meetings about homelessness, someone might want to access it because she is specifically interested in homeless women, or because he is looking for patterns of interruptions of speech in public meetings, or because she is looking for ethnographic strategies for talking to public officials, none of which was the reason you wrote the book. There should, though, be terms in the index so these anonymous readers can find what they are looking for.

The convention in scholarly publishing is that the author is responsible for doing the index or paying for someone else to do it. That this piece of the production cycle is left to (forced upon?) the author probably has a long history related to the assumption that the author, usually an indexing newbie, has the best understanding of his or her own material. Whatever the genesis, almost all academic publishers leave the indexing to the author. You can do it yourself, persuade a friend or student for love or money to do it for you, or hire an indexer. The publisher will often share a list of indexers they have worked with if you ask. If you pay for an index, the cost can currently range between $1 and $5 per text page in your book. So the index for a 300 page book can run you over $1,000. Most authors chose to do their own. And grumble all the way.

Can you do without one? Not really. Academic libraries use the presence of an index as one of their criteria for deciding which books to purchase. No index = far fewer library sales. That's not a good tradeoff.

How about a shortcut? Surely there must be software that can find all of these words and identify which page they're on. Of course there are, and that will get you half way. If you're a decent writer, you use synonyms for your key concepts. You use metaphors. You describe concepts without using the word for that concept. A word search program will find every occurrence of that *word*, but won't necessarily find the *concepts* if expressed in other ways. Nor can it create a hierarchy of terms for you, linking related ones (homeless women, homeless policy, violence against homeless, homeless shelters), all of which would be subentries of "homeless" in a good index. That part is manual, too.

The best shortcut is advanced preparation. If you do a first draft of the index while writing your manuscript and turn it in with the rest of the book, it gives a copyeditor a chance to edit it. Keep the page numbers from the original manuscript on your copy of the index you turned in, and you should be able to convert the page numbers fairly quickly and mechanically when you get the typeset proofs. Or do the index while the production team is working on other parts of your book before indexing time arrives. In this way, your only task is finding page numbers, not creating the intellectual content. Even if you've decided that you are hiring an outside indexer, develop a list of preferred terms for them to include. It helps guide a professional indexer's work if they know what terms the expert on the material thinks are important.

Teaching you how to index is beyond the scope of this work. There are whole books on how to do it (see appendix A), but the place we usually send people to is the Chicago Manual of Style chapter on indexing.

Finally, the production phase is done. The project manager tells you that the book has gone to the printer and you should have a printed copy in your hands in a few weeks. Time to wrap this one up and move on to the next project. Not so fast! What about...marketing?

Huh? Marketing? Not my job! But it is, at least partially. On to the next chapter...

Chapter 10

Marketing Your Work

Done. Done. DONE!!!

Time for a happy dance! Your journal editor tells you the article is "in press" for the March issue. Or the book is finally off to the printer with a promise that you'll have the first copy off the press in a few weeks. Time to call it a wrap and start on the next item on your list, the To Do list that you've been carefully avoiding while you have been responsibly taking care of production details to ensure the process flows smoothly.

I hate to tell you what follows. It will ruin your whole day.

Let's take your journal article, for example. We already determined there are 100,000 journals out there and 1.8 million articles published annually. If you did a good job on your title, abstract, and keywords, people who come looking for your topic are likely to find you. But that's the passive approach. You want people talking about your article, reacting to it, inviting you to keynote their conference, asking you to write a book on it. That won't come from waiting for someone to find you. You need to be proactive in getting the word out about the word you're getting out.

Essentials of Publishing Qualitative Research by Mitchell Allen.
137–145. © 2016 Left Coast Press, Inc. All rights reserved.

Marketing Your Published Article

An effective journal publisher will be doing some of this for you. Most have active news feeds to the electronic information sources in the disciplines in which they publish, advertising the contents of a new issue of each journal as it comes out. Some will offer free articles, either permanently or on a limited basis, as an incentive for readers to explore their journal. Journal publishers will also give away sample copies at conferences in the hopes that attendees will take them back to their librarians and insist they subscribe. All will post the Tables of Contents on their website with title, abstract, and keywords.

While it may feel uncomfortable, you will want to "market" your article as well. If you have a website or a university repository, post the accepted draft (see chapter 11 about green open access rules) on it. Other sites like ResearchGate or Academia.edu allow you to post your work as well and announce it to people following you. Make sure your professional community knows you have accounts on those sites and find a way of getting them to follow you (by following them, of course). If you want to influence the movers and shakers, find their email addresses and send them a copy of the article, asking for their feedback. Again, you need to check publishers' rules on this. Most academics are too shy to go on listservs to announce they've published a new article, but you can reach a lot of people that way. Record a 60 second blurb about your piece and its importance; post it on an appropriate YouTube channel. Getting social media involved is effective; produce Facebook/LinkedIn/Twitter posts announcing your latest publication. Your university has a public relations office that is always looking for things to highlight from faculty research. Figure out an important or interesting hook to your subject and tell them about it. Send an email to your address book offering a copy of your article to anyone who wants to read it and asking them to let other people know. These steps will help your article stand out from the 1,799,999 others published this year.

Longer term strategies are equally simple and equally effective. Cite yourself. Yes, it's uncomfortable, but you can't guarantee that someone reading one article will know that you've written other relevant pieces. Arrange that your next couple of professional talks are on the theme of your recently published paper. Offer to write a short guest piece for a blog on this topic. Set up a talk at the local university brown bag lunch or the local chapter of your professional society on this topic. Your stuff is good; it's even better if someone discovers and reads it.

Table 10.1: Marketing Tools for the Entrepreneurial Academic

- ► Announce your new publication on your website, Facebook, Twitter accounts
- ► Make sure you have website, Facebook, and Twitter accounts
- ► Create a separate website, Facebook page, Twitter account specifically for your book and populate it regularly
- ► Send an email to your entire personal email list (even crazy Aunt Gracie) announcing your new publication
- ► Post links and the publications, if possible, on ResearchGate and Academia. edu
- ► Send an announcement to the listservs you are on, Yahoo or Google Plus groups
- ► Send announcements to your professional association newsletter, section newsletters, your departmental newsletter
- ► Give some local talks about your work and mention your publication
- ► Make sure your next several conference presentations are about your recently published work
- ► Bring copies of the paper or flyers on the book to distribute at those presentations
- ► Cite yourself in future work
- ► Selectively send copies of your article, even your book, to "people that matter"
- ► Find a popular angle from your publication and feed it to your university public relations office

Marketing Your New Book

- *They never promoted my book to anthropologists. Not surprising it only sold 124 copies.*
- *It was never reviewed.*
- *They left my book out of their catalog.*

If you've just finished your book, the need to market is even greater. After all, you're paid royalties on the number of copies you sell and your career trajectory is determined by how widely your ideas are read and cited. If you leave it to the publisher to try to sell your book, you're not maximizing your possibilities. And your publisher knows that your passionate expression of your ideas is the best way to sell your book.

Remember that your publisher is producing 10 or 50 or 500 other books at the same time as yours. There are some general procedures they will be following to sell your book. That is how they make money. Their process has started long before the book hits the warehouse, possibly even before you finished writing it.

The publisher prepared a Book Information Form (often called a tipsheet or advanced book information form, ABI) for the institutional buyers—university libraries, library wholesalers, international distributors, bookstore wholesalers—that provides basic information about your book. This is a crucial piece for you to know about because the title, price, and marketing message are usually codified in this document. Find out from your editor when it is going to be produced and ask to see it. This piece is usually written by the marketing manager responsible for your book. In addition to writing yours, she probably has to do a dozen others. And, of course, she knows nothing about you or your book except some brief notes from your editor. Follow my advice about the importance of networking... it's time to make a new BFF. Have a conversation with the marketing manager, then write down what you think are the most important things to highlight. Cover key phrases to use, major sales points, major competitors, who your idealized reader is, and what such readers can get out of the book. If the marketing manager has this in hand at the time she writes your Book Information Form, she's likely to crib from your work rather than start from scratch, and you've helped define the way your book is presented to the public.

With the Book Information Form done, which contains most of the information the marketing department will use to advertise the book, they will go through their normal marketing procedures. At many publishing houses, the marketing manager will be asked to write up a formal marketing plan for her boss. The plan will include what catalogs to include the book in, what conferences to send it to, what journals to review it in, what publications to advertise it in, social media to hype it on. You want to have a chat with her before she finalizes the plan to give her input on her ideas and to provide your own.

Often that step is a more formal one. Usually about the time the book goes into production, the marketing manager will send you an Author Questionnaire asking for feedback on these items. Our questionnaire asks about your social media accounts, your university press office, the key review journals in your field, your professional affiliations, what mailing lists you might have access to, your media experience, what conferences you regularly attend (see appendix B). Take some time with this questionnaire and provide as much information as you can. It will be a long term record that the marketers can use to help sell your book. Much of the information you've already gathered for your book proposal. Even if you fill it to overflowing with information, you still want to have that conversation with the marketing manager. A personal relationship always trumps the information.

Then keep in regular touch with the marketing manager about their activities and yours. If you're going to a conference, let her know, preferably many weeks in advance of the date. With adequate warning, they will equip you with flyers and a sample copy of the book to display at your session. If they have a conference on their website calendar, maybe you should consider attending and work with your publisher to arrange a book signing or other event at the booth. If you advertise your work on a listserv or write a blog post about it, make sure the marketing manager knows so that she can forward it to their mailing lists and post a link on their website as well. If they produce a new catalog, ask for a handful of copies to drop off in your department lounge. Direct marketing is more and more done through emails to appropriate audiences. Ask to see any email campaigns that have gone out; better yet, ask to get on the appropriate email and direct mail lists early on.

Some authors have found it useful to create a separate website, Facebook page, Twitter account, and/or blog specifically for their book. In coordination with the publisher, you can place various bits of the book on these sites, announcing each improvement on your social media networks to draw interest to the book. As articles and postings come out, you create a living presence for the book going forward, a place for you to add further thoughts, post reviewers' and other readers' comments, provide more contextual information about your work. Links back and forth to the publisher's social media will allow you to increase your reach by using their networks as well. The danger here is that these web locations need to be regularly fed with new material. Nothing looks sadder than a website that hasn't been updated in three or four years.

Book Signings and Other Events

Back in the good old days, the publication of a new book was cause for a party in your honor at the conference of your major profession- al organization. If they had 10 new books, often they had 10 parties. A rented suite was stocked with beer and snacks; or sometimes they arranged a rolling tray of the perfunctory wine, fruit, cheese, and bread in the exhibit hall. A good time was had by all. This event would be paralleled at your hometown, where someone would fly out from the publishing house and host a reception for you in conjunc- tion with a signing at a local bookstore. Of course, if you believed all those 1940s movies, everyone wore ball gowns and tuxes to go out each evening, too.

It still happens at some conferences, at some bookstores, and with some books. But not so often and not so lavishly. If your book wins a major association award, you can lobby the publisher to do it up into a big event. But the publisher will not always agree. Book signings at conferences are much easier—after all, the publisher gets to sell more books that way. They just need to make sure to send more copies of the book to the conference and advertise the event so people to come by for a signed copy. You can help by announcing this event to your own networks, by talking with your marketing manager to make sure enough books were sent, and reminding her to advertise the book signing to the publisher's mailing lists at the appropriate time. And, if you really want a party, offer to pay half the costs if the publisher will pony up the rest. Much more of this event-making now takes place because of the author's initiative than the publisher's. So, if you like throwing parties, throw one and see how much you can get your publisher to cooperate in advertising, supporting, and paying for it.

Getting Your Publisher to Do More for Your Book

Start by having realistic expectations. If the publisher produces 1,500 books a year and has 12 marketing managers, you can roughly calculate the workload each one has been saddled with. If you did your research right, you know what the publisher will do as a standard advertising package for an average book. You can supplement the base model by doing all you can to support your marketing manager's work, by sending her information on opportunities that arise—your speaking engagements, small conferences, mailing lists that come your way—and by reminding her of the marketing opportunities you sent her last month. Being a fount of useful information is always a good idea. The easier you make the marketing manager's job, the more likely she is to do it for you.

This activity won't last forever. The same dirty dozen marketing managers will have 1,500 more books to market next year, too. So be particularly active in the months preceding publication of your book and the year following it.

Remember also that there are parts of the publisher's marketing activities that you never see. The book information form goes out to the institutional buyers, places that you never hear about but which populate the world's databases and bring orders from libraries and bookstores throughout the world. They also create a home for your book on their website, put it in their catalogs and other flyers going to mailing lists and disciplines that you might never see, arrange to transport it with them to a variety of conferences they attend, create a list of places to send review copies. They likely have international branches or distributors in various places on the planet and feed all the information they have gathered to their representatives in Korea, Kolkota, and Copenhagen.

If you're not getting follow through on the opportunities you provided or think that the level of marketing has dropped off too quickly, check in with your marketing manager and ask what they've done for you lately. At the same time, tell them what you've done for them.

With so many books to market, it's easy for her to forget yours without gentle but persistent reminders. If your marketing manager is being unresponsive, try to bring the acquiring editor into the discussion as well. She, after all, is the champion of your book within the publishing house. She wants it to succeed as much as you do. And don't be surprised at disappointment. There are campaigns and events that don't produce the way you or the publisher expects, despite the best intentions and best efforts.

Ways You Can Help Your Publisher

There are some specific ways in which you can help their efforts and, in fact, increase them by giving them more tools to work with:

Blurbs. It always helps to sell a book if someone well-known says it is good. Most publishers try to obtain these brief quotes for the back cover and for their marketing. You can help. Suggest names of people who are central to various networks you are trying to reach. If you know them, or know someone who knows them, try to make the contact yourself. If not, try to provide the marketing manager with contact information so she can ask for the endorsement. It's sure nice to see them when they come in. But remember, the average academic book cover only has room for three or four quotes. Getting ten endorsements only means that you don't use half of them and waste someone's time in writing them. The timing of getting the endorsements is important—you want them in hand before the cover gets designed and before the seasonal catalog announcing your new book gets prepared.

Mailing lists. Your book won't be read by "everybody" but hopefully will be of interest to a chunk of people in your subfield, people who belong to the organizations you belong to, read the journals you read, attend the conferences you attend. So make sure the marketing person can reach all the people you know. Dig out all those attendee lists from the conferences you've attended on your topic. Pull down the mailing list of the special interest group on your topic at your major professional association. Weed through your own address books and compile a list of people who might buy your book. Those names are invaluable to your publisher and they should be able to use them to sell your book.

Review journals. The publisher will likely have a list of general review journals in your field, but you can help fine tune it with more specialized journals, newsletters, and other media that do reviews. If you have the time to research the name and contact info of the book review editor, she will have no reason not to send a copy. Warning: Almost no academic books get reviewed by the *New York Times* or *Time Magazine.* Unless your cousin works there, don't bother suggesting it.

In addition to supporting their efforts, there are many things you can do on your own. So follow my advice above on advertising your new journal article for your book as well: use your own social media, post announcements on listservs, write blog pieces, deliver conference papers based on your book. Announce the publication of your book to your professional organization and to your personal mailing and email lists. Run workshops on your topic, if it is appropriate. Talk to your university public relations office.

And Finally...

...recognize that no article or book has *ever* been fully marketed. There will always be additional avenues unexplored, opportunities unsnatched. Between your publisher's professional marketing package, your additions to it through feeding them opportunities you uncover, and your own work at marketing your work, you can maximize the reach of the message to potential audiences. But you and your publisher will never truly exhaust all of your potential audiences or the opportunities to reach them.

Chapter 11

The Brave New World of Electronic Publishing

There has been enough noise generated over the rapid migration to electronic publishing to deafen all of us. Every tome about the state of academia, every academic conference, and a constant thump in the blogosphere seem to address this topic. What does all this mean for you, for your publication strategies, for your readership, for your writing future?

The risk of trying to prognosticate the future is immense. I have a copy of a *Harper's Magazine* article from 1856 that accurately predicted the invention of air travel. But airships consisted of hot air balloons powered by steam engines. Like that article, this chapter should be worth a good laugh in a few years.

The simple answer to the question might be shocking. Basically, nothing has changed. Computers are not new. They've been around since before most of us were born. Archaeologists have even found complex calculating devices dating back to Roman times (that's 2,000 years). Most junior scholars have always had websites to look at and emails to write and receive.

The same is true of your publications. The journals you read today generally arrive electronically. But they're still journals, usually structured in quarterly issues and consisting of research articles

The reading devices may change, but the writing hasn't yet.

with abstracts at the beginning and bibliography at the end. This is becoming the pattern with scholarly books, too: your college library is investing ever more in electronic versions of books that you can download in your pajamas at home. But these books still have tables of contents, eight chapters, and bibliographies.

So relax. Until universities change their reward system, you needn't worry about changing your reading and writing habits away from the article and book. And you know how fast university systems change, don't you? As long as articles and books are valued, the old system will be largely unchanged, though the opportunities to produce other kinds of work will expand with the technology if you choose to experiment with it.

Open Access

One thing that is different in the current publishing ecology is the ability to publish something "open access," that is, freely available on the web for anyone and everyone to read. The movement is largely driven by the battles between large commercial publishers and large university libraries over pricing of their goods. Can we do away with the commercial publishing sector completely so that scholarship is truly free to everyone who wants to read it? And that includes not only your colleagues, but your students, people in other research areas who might stumble across your work, even your mom and dad who are proud of their daughter the professor. And, every scholar hopes, the audience will include the curious non-academic reader sitting at his or her desk in Hong Kong or Hanover or Houston. What a wonderful utopian world that would be, a global public audience for your writing! Most of the battle to date has been over making journals open access, but the same principles apply to books.

"Open" Access Is Not Free

Many of its proponents speak of open access with a religious fervor. It is a way of breaking the stranglehold of large commercial journal publishers who hide your published work from potential readers behind expensive firewalls. It is a democratizing movement, where your scholarly work is available to any and all interested readers for free on the net. These prophets are right about the problem. There's only one issue with their solution: open access systems are not free. Someone pays for them.

It costs money to edit, to typeset, to host journals and books, to protect legal rights of creators, to publicize articles and books to those interested in the work, and to administer all of these systems, whether paper or electronic. Converting everything to eBooks won't solve the problem: the cost of printing scholarly material is only a small fraction of the overall cost. If publishers are no longer responsible for these other tasks using their own capital, someone else will have to perform them. Will the author be forced to subsidize his or her own work, or will professional organizations extract these costs from your organization dues? The most likely candidate to manage these tasks is your college library, except for one issue: it is subject to vagaries and budget uncertainty that plague all universities. If you're looking for a system that will ensure your book or article is available in perpetuity, it is a bit unnerving that the task rests with a branch of your university that must *always* have the funds to keep your writings in print. If there's a budget shortfall, do they cut the qualitative journal they host before the one on cancer research?

Proponents can show many open access publications that work effectively today. Their founders should be proud. But they still represent a small fraction of the content output and still are reliant on much volunteer labor. The Danish journal *Qualitative Studies* recently posted on its website,

> We regret to inform you that the journal Qualitative Studies is not able to receive manuscripts at the moment. The journal has been based on the voluntary work of the editors, which is no longer possible to uphold, and we are now considering how to develop the journal in the future. All manuscripts already in our system will of course be handled normally. (ojs.statsbiblioteket.dk/index. php/qual/index)

What happens when open access systems become responsible for the 100,000 academic journals and hundreds of thousands of new books published each year? Where will the money come to hire all the copyeditors, typesetters, and proofreaders to polish your work? The systems will also require IT people needed to handle all this material, staffers who are far more expensive than print shop and warehouse workers. Lots of them. The cost of system maintenance, security, and system upgrades are not cheap either, probably more expensive than maintaining a warehouse. As these costs go up, will open access require you to pay to help cover them? These key economic questions have not been resolved.

The other issue about open access is that it does not provide the most important thing a publisher does for you—publicity (hence the origin of the term). When your carefully crafted work is posted on the server along with thousands of other works on the same topic from hundreds of other authors, many of whom lack the necessary professional credentials, what will draw attention to your project? Under the current system, a publisher has the responsibility to tell the world how good it is. And they do (see chapter 10). Under an open access system, that becomes your job. Thus, the most important works are likely to be the ones promulgated by the best academic self-promoters. I can guess how well you already like those colleagues. Or even worse, the attention will go to someone who has no academic credentials but is good at publicity, even if he sucks at doing careful research. You already see many of them inhabiting the web; expect that to increase.

Commercial journal publishers have attempted to coopt the open access movement by making articles free to readers by charging the author. This **gold open access** model allows the author to pay for the privilege of removing the firewall for their publication. Costs can run from a few hundred dollars to several thousand. Not a big deal for a large med school NIH-sponsored project, just a few more dollars added to the multimillion dollar grant proposal. But for an independent scholar in the humanities or a graduate student? The system seems to reward the wealthiest scholarly areas at the expense of the poorest. Not a democratizing movement at all.

The other drive for open access has come from government, which wants "the people" to be able to access the work funded by their tax dollars. Thus, new regulations on making research findings public have been promulgated in a number of countries, including by several US federal agencies. Many universities have similar regulations, requiring public availability of their scholars' output. You might like the idea of putting your work as open access documents in your university repository, but recognize that some scholarly journals and book publishers won't publish it if it is available on the web for free. The publishing industry has established a set of rules to preserve the exclusivity of their material. These **green open access** rules almost always prevent the author from posting the published version; rather, preliminary unedited, pre-typeset versions are allowed in these repositories. Not particularly useful if you wish to cite the page number and date of the published version. Often the publisher will establish an embargo of a year or two before the material can be made available in these repositories.

While commercial publishers receive most of the criticism in this battle over control of scholarly publications, there have emerged some players who truly wear black hats. A host of new journals have popped up, many based in China and India, who will volunteer to publish your article for a fee much smaller than Springer or Sage. These **predatory journals** will often not have editors or editorial boards, but will have titles sounding like traditional scholarly publications and will promise speedy, inexpensive, and open access publication. For example, Open Research Network launched 86 journals simultaneously in the spring of 2013. The journals, with titles like ORN Journal of African Studies and Development and ORN Journal of Agricultural Biotechnology and Sustainable Development, were listed on their website, but there was no list of journal editors or editorial boards, nor any evidence of peer review. It would cost you $300 per accepted article to publish in an Open Research Network journal, with no guarantee that the academic community would give you any credit for this publication (Scholarly Open Access Network 2013).

To help monitor this flood of new, sketchy journals, Jeffrey Beall, librarian for the University of Colorado, developed a list of predatory open access journals, *scholarlyoa.com*, whose peer review processes are questionable and who charge to publish in their journals. This list has become a watchword for academic librarians and should be for you as well before you submit an article to a journal you've not heard of.

Do-It-Yourself Electronic Publications

There are good reasons to considering publishing your own work in electronic form. Perhaps you are using a lot of multimedia pieces. Perhaps it is very long or very short, not the traditional length of a book or article. Perhaps you wish to include not only your description and analysis, but the whole project—interview data, observations, field notes, photos, email correspondence—which would allow others to use your data to do their own studies. Perhaps you are convinced that your piece won't appeal to journal editors or book publishers. Perhaps you just want more flexibility to do it your way without having to compromise with outsiders who want you to fit their publishing models. These are all good reasons to try the do-it-yourself path.

There are some things you need to think about before you start:

Technical expertise. No one likes a badly designed publication or website, if you go that route. Do you have the skill to put it together yourself, or the skill to be able to direct someone technically more competent to do so? Do you or does your technowhiz know how to make it attractive on a variety of devices, from small phones to large desktop screens? If you want it to be interactive, will that interactivity work on a variety of systems and browsers? Do you know how much it will cost to do that? Fortunately, there are a growing number of production services who will do some of this for you for a fee.

Longevity. Yes, this technowhiz friend can set up the electronic publication for you, but how will you make sure it stays active and up-to-date for the long term. This has both a technical component— who knew a decade ago that everything you do needs to be readable on a phone screen?—and a content component. We've all seen websites that were set up in 2010 and not touched since then. Quaint. Funny. Useless. If you create something like this, it needs to be updated and made available for the long haul. Are you going to commit to update the site for years, even decades, into the future. If not, do you have the money to pay someone else to do it and a platform that you know will be around for a long time?

Discoverability. Having a website isn't worth it if no one can find you. Sending out an email to all your friends telling them it exists will do for the short run, but not for the long term. Do you know how to maximize your location on web browsers? Do you have the keywords in place that will cause people to find you when they're looking for something that fits your site? Do you have enough links to enough other related websites that people will find you by finding others? There's work involved there, both in making the links and asking others to look at your site. In traditional publishing, it would be called marketing.

Copyright. Commercial presses spend a lot of money trying to keep their products behind a firewall so that they can't be stolen and repurposed by others. Is this a concern? What happens if someone takes your data and uses it for something completely inappropriate?

Production quality, a solid distribution network, long-term sustainability, advertising the availability of your product, rights protection. Guess what? You have become a publisher.

Your Electronic Publishing Future

When I point to the two main themes of the current change in academic publishing, know that this might not represent your future. But they come in an opposition pair: 'aggregation' and 'disaggregation.'

Aggregation has been occurring in the academic publishing world for a while now. When your college librarian looks to add another journal to the archive, the first place they look is to the available collections of journals. Large journal publishers like Springer, Elsevier, and Sage all have them. So do non-profits like JSTOR and Project Muse. It's the Walmart approach, buy more cheaply in bulk. Each of these publishers offers collections of journals for a small fraction of the cost of buying each individually. More and more, large publishers and third party vendors, such as EBSCO and Proquest, are doing the same for books. Buy 3,000 education or sociology books from 200 publishers at a small fraction of what the individual books would cost. These are offered to libraries in a variety of programs called things like patron-driven acquisitions and short-term loans. Publishers who don't have their own proprietary systems are somewhat skeptical that the money they get out of these aggregate programs matches what they might have secured in the old one-book-one-library system. These aggregations are now being offered to individuals—JSTOR has one, for example—and are only going to increase in the future. If you're not affiliated with a university, you can plug into a large collection for a fee.

What does this mean for you the scholar? In theory, this creates much greater access as more libraries have more material available for you. It also might shift your focus. If your library has the Sage collection but not the Taylor & Francis one, you might read and reference Sage articles more than T&F ones, whether or not they are the right articles for your piece. As a writer, this also should be a boon to you—if your articles and books are available in more libraries, more people will read your work.

The danger of greater access was discussed earlier in this book. If your library contains all 1.8 million articles published this year and the 1.8 million published last year, how are readers going to find *your* work. It will make the titles you choose, the abstracts you write, the keywords you use, the marketing of your own work ever more critical.

Simultaneous with the move toward aggregation of publishing, has been the move toward disaggregation. Why should your library subscribe to *Qualitative Inquiry* when all you really want from it is two specific articles this year and maybe none next year? Why not just access those articles and forget the whole subscription thing. Or just pull the one chapter out of a book without having to buy and read the whole thing. If all you wanted from this book was information on how to get your article accepted, you still had to purchase another 100 pages on other topics to obtain it. Why not just buy that chapter?

Or why not grab the one useful table that you need from the marketing chapter? Or access the references to make sure you didn't miss something important in writing your own piece? The other trend in academic publishing is that one, allowing you to obtain just what you want without having to include the rest of what the author wanted you to read. All journal publishers with an online presence will allow you to purchase a single article without subscribing to the publication. Many book publishers sell their edited books by the chapter now, and there are some third party organizations, like University Readers or Academicpub.com, who will do the same for you. Many publishers have selected sections of their books available on Google Books.

So, if you can now access information in all shapes and sizes, from a single table to the entire collection of works of hundreds of publishers in a single field, what is keeping the old system in place—where you write articles or books, have them reviewed, revised, and published? You can thank the conservativism of the tenure system for that. Those Faculty Evaluation Committees still look at your CV and assess the number and worth of all those articles and books in order to give you the promotion and tenure. As long as that system stays intact, you will be pushed to produce publishable articles and books, no matter how they're sliced and diced when they get into the hands of the publisher.

That's not to say there isn't some change in that system that works to the advantage of qualitative researchers. Some enlightened universities are beginning to realize that community-based researchers who are eradicating poverty or building community health capacities don't really have the time to put it all down in an article for *The Lancet*. Some performance scholars can submit the video of their two act ethnodrama instead of PDFs of yet another article. But each case is still a battle. The system is very conservative and might take additional generations to change.

If the Center No Longer Holds

But what if the tenure system gets abolished or transformed? (Yes, assistant professors, you are allowed to have nightmares about this.) What would that do to the publishing landscape? The same two terms apply here—aggregation and disaggregation. In one direction, I would expect to see an increase in making full projects of research available, including all your field notes, code books, and multimedia content.

Bigger works. In the other direction, I would expect an increase of Scholarship by Tweet, smaller, more frequent packets of information from your research, some of it while the research is still taking place. Smaller works. Both directions present opportunities and dangers. If these products become accepted as valued academic work, the infrastructures to support them are already in place.

And who knows what else? Free exchanges between scholars and their publics on open websites? Google swallowing up the entire output of the global academy? There are plenty of utopian and dystopian scenarios out there. To avoid the steam-powered flying balloons, I'll skip any more predictions.

Now you can roll over and go back to sleep. The tenure system will be with us for a while yet, I promise.

Chapter 12

Coda

Here's where I get to sum up and provide you with pearls of wisdom that you'll carry through your academic career. I can sum the lessons in this book up really quickly:

> Academic publishing is socially constructed; treat it that way. Do the research about publishing the way you do the rest of your research; treat people in your publishing interactions the same way you do as an empathetic qualitative scholar, and all will be fine.

You've already spent too much time reading this. You should be out there writing things to publish and networking with gatekeepers to get them published. I've given you the best advice I have.

So stop stalling. Put the book down. Now! And get back to work.

Key Resources about Publishing

Books about Finding the Right Publisher

Belcher, Wendy Laura, WRITING YOUR JOURNAL ARTICLE IN 12 WEEKS (Sage, 2009). If you want to read 350 pages on how to write 20, this is the book for you.

Derricourt, Robin, AN AUTHOR'S GUIDE TO SCHOLARLY PUBLISHING (Princeton University Press, 1996). This and the Luey book are the best general discussions of the practicalities of scholarly publishing.

Fortunato, Alfred, and Susan Rabiner, THINKING LIKE YOUR EDITOR: How to Write Great Serious Nonfiction and Get It Published (Norton, 2003). Rabiner, a past editorial director of Basic Books, gives detailed guidelines on how to publish for the trade (bookstore) audience and find an agent.

Germano, William, GETTING IT PUBLISHED, 2nd ed. (University of Chicago Press, 2008). Guidelines for working with editors by one who ran Routledge. Includes electronic publishing issues.

Luey, Beth, HANDBOOK FOR ACADEMIC AUTHORS, 5th ed. (Cambridge University Press, 2009). Practical advice on approaching publishers and on the writing process.

Smedley, Christine et al. GETTING YOUR BOOK PUBLISHED (Sage, 1993). Older but excellent brief guide for academic social scientists coauthored by Sage's editorial staff, including me.

Thyer, Bruce A., SUCCESSFUL PUBLISHING IN SCHOLARLY JOURNALS (Sage, 1994). A brief and very pragmatic guide for academic authors on how to negotiate the world of publishing in academic journals.

How to Turn a Dissertation into a Book

Luey, Beth, editor. REVISING YOUR DISSERTATION: Advice from Leading Editors, updated ed. (University of California Press, 2008). Tips from those in the publishing industry about how to turn your dissertation into a book.

Germano, William, FROM DISSERTATION TO BOOK (University of Chicago Press, 2005). Another take on the same topic.

Harman, Eleanor, Ian Montagnes, Siobhan McMenemy, and Chris Bucci, editors, THE THESIS AND THE BOOK, 2nd ed. (University of Toronto Press, 2003). Seven essays from different authors on how to turn a thesis into a book.

Books on Writing Qualitative Research

Becker, Howard, WRITING FOR SOCIAL SCIENTISTS, 2nd ed. (University of Chicago Press, 2007). Tons of useful tips for academic writing from a legendary figure in qualitative research.

Goodall, H. L. Jr., WRITING QUALITATIVE INQUIRY (Left Coast, 2008). Covers writing creative non-fiction, but also professional issues in writing experimental texts and being a public intellectual.

Richardson, Laurel, WRITING STRATEGIES: Reaching Diverse Audiences (Sage, 1990). Laurel Richardson's explication of different ways to work with qualitative material for different audiences.

Wolcott, Harry F., WRITING UP QUALITATIVE RESEARCH, 3rd ed. (Sage, 2009). Wolcott's book is like floating on a gentle river. When you arrive, you realize how much good advice on writing he has for qualitative researchers.

Technical Writing/Editing/Indexing Resources

Achtert, Walter S., and Joseph Garibaldi, THE MLA MANUAL OF STYLE, 3rd ed. (Modern Language Association, 2008).

Butcher, Judith, COPY-EDITING, 4th ed. (Cambridge University Press, 2006).

CHICAGO MANUAL OF STYLE, 16th ed. (University of Chicago Press, 2010).

Eisohn, Amy, THE COPYEDITOR'S HANDBOOK, 3rd ed. (University of California Press, 2011).

Miller, Casey, and Kate Swift, THE HANDBOOK OF NONSEXIST WRITING: FOR WRITERS, EDITORS, AND SPEAKERS, 2nd ed. (iUniverse, 2001).

Mulvany, Nancy, INDEXING BOOKS, 2nd ed. (University of Chicago Press, 2005).

Strong, William S., THE COPYRIGHT BOOK: A PRACTICAL GUIDE, 6th ed. (MIT Press, 2014).

Strunk, W., Jr., and E. B. White, THE ELEMENTS OF STYLE, 3rd ed. (Macmillan, 1979).

Left Coast Author's Marketing Questionnaire

Dear Left Coast Author:

Thank you for taking the time to complete this questionnaire. It is an important opportunity for you to provide input into our marketing campaign for your new book.

Our standard marketing plan includes sending direct mail catalogs, flyers, and postcards; sending electronic announcements and postings; displaying books at conferences; and sending review copies to journals, key distributors, and other relevant publications and media. That is, we should already know about the major audiences and outlets in your field—that your ethnography should be on display at the American Anthropological Association, that a review copy of your archaeological theory book should be sent to *American Antiquity*, or that the NAME needs to know about your book on museum exhibits. That means your expertise will be particularly helpful in identifying smaller or more specialized subfields or interdisciplinary groups, providing personal contacts you may have for endorsements and other publicity, telling us about special presentations or talks you are giving that might offer a marketing opportunity, and so on. We encourage you to take an active role in marketing, and welcome your ideas.

Essentials of Publishing Qualitative Research by Mitchell Allen.
163–166. © 2016 Left Coast Press, Inc. All rights reserved.

Please remember that with our marketing experience also comes knowledge about where our money is most effectively spent, and that the budget isn't infinite, so we may not choose to implement all of your suggestions.

Our international distributors—Eurospan in Europe, Africa, and the Middle East, and Footprint in Australia and New Zealand—are also receptive to your marketing ideas in those territories.

1. Contact Information. It is important that we are able to get in touch with you with production and marketing questions and events. Please supply your contact information: include more than one location if relevant, including home and office, and known dates of travel in the next twelve months and contact information during travel (if available).

Travel information:

2. Web Sites. Include your professional homepage URL, if you have one, and those of contributors, if appropriate, so we can provide links to your book on our web site; and any other relevant sites (professional organizations, etc.) that might be willing to include a link to your book.

3. Professional Information: We should already have the biographical sketch you submitted with your manuscript, as well as a copy of your C.V. If not, please send these to us, as there is often good marketing information there that you might not have thought of. Among the personal information we are looking for is:

- Universities you have attended (and departments/degrees) for alumni magazine notices
- Professional memberships; other honors and offices relevant to the book's promotion
- Foreign editions of your previous books, so we can pursue translation rights
- Other key activities, honors, positions, publications

If this is an edited book, you might canvass your contributors for this information as well.

4. Endorsements. Endorsements by other well-known scholars help us sell your book by giving the reader more confidence in its quality.

Please list the names (and contact information if possible) of at least three people whose endorsements you feel might help sell the book. Identify those you know personally. Let us know whom you would like us to contact and whom you will contact yourself. It is often quickest and easiest to obtain endorsements from those who have already read some or all of your manuscript.

5. Electronic Marketing. Electronic communication has become an essential component of marketing. Please give us the following information:

- Which listserves, blogs, and other online discussion forums do you monitor?
- Are you willing to post an electronic announcement of publication when the book comes out?
- Can you share your email address book with us so that we can announce your book to your contacts?
- Do you have access to any lists of email addresses of interested professionals so that we may notify them of publication of your book?
- Can you give us the details of your Twitter, Facebook, LinkedIn or other social networking account so we can link book information to you?

6. Audiences. Again, we should already know the major audience(s) for your book. Your suggestions for more specialized audiences will be most helpful, including:

- The specialized subfields that you feel your book will appeal to;
- The disciplines outside your own in which you hope to find readership;
- The characteristics of non-specialists who might pick up your book;
- The level of students/courses for which your book is appropriate;
- Specific instructors (including their college addresses) who are likely to adopt your book for their classes.

9. Mailing Lists. Targeted direct mail is an important marketing strategy, and we have access to mailing lists for many major national and international associations. Can you also obtain for us, or direct us to, other lists we may not know about, including subsections in your discipline, newsletters, specialized journals, conference attendees, and other informal networks that are likely to want to receive flyers on your book? Please include contact information whenever possible. If you have a personal mailing list or address lists from conferences you have recently attended, those would be most helpful. We need full addresses and particularly email addresses in order to be able to use them.

10. Book Reviews. In addition to those listed above, tell us which specialized academic and professional journals you believe are likely to review your book (including journals based outside the U.S.). Include names and addresses of book review editors if possible.

11. Affiliated Publicity. Will the press office(s) of the university or organization with which you are affiliated help publicize your book? Are there journalists, editors or media professionals you have been in contact with in the past who might want to feature your work?

12. Conferences. Which professional conferences do you attend regularly? Are there any specialized meetings you will be attending or know about to which we might be able to send the books and advertising material? Please include conferences outside the U.S.

13. Book Events. Let us know if you are planning to conduct book signings or delivering lectures based on your book. We can usually coordinate with the sponsor or bookstore to make sure there are books to be sold there. If not, let us know if you would like us to send you flyers to display at the event.

14. Anything Else We Should Know?

Notes

Chapter 1: Inside the Black Box

1. Though this is changing. Some online open access pan-disciplinary journals use publisher staff members as the decision makers for selecting articles.

2. I will use female pronouns throughout when referring to publishing personnel. Most people working in publishing are women and, as with most woman-dominated professions, they are underpaid and undervalued. Not surprisingly, the exception is that most of the people working in the penthouse are male, though I had the experience of working for a series of talented women publishers for my first 20 years in the business.

Chapter 3: Finding the Right Journal

1. These 12,000 include 5,300 social science and 2,500 arts and humanities journals. wokinfo.com/citationconnection/realfacts/ #regional, accessed March, 6, 2015.

2. Eigenfactor.org uses a longer time frame and a different algorithm; Scimoagojr.com, proprietary to Elsevier, is based on their journal database Scopus; SNIP (Source Normalized Impact per Paper) corrects for differences between disciplines www. journalmetrics.com/; H-Index looks at scholar's overall productivity across all publications, based on Google Scholar www. southampton.ac.uk/library/research/bibliometrics/factsheet

03-hindex-gs.pdf. A nice summary of these alternate systems is available from the journal publisher Elsevier, cdn.elsevier.com/assets/pdf_file/0020/131816/Understanding-the-Publishing-Process.pdf

Chapter 4: Writing, Reviewing, and Revising Your Article

1. You could start with a book in this series, van den Hoonaard and van den Hoonaard (2012), and Martin Tolich's (2015) *Qualitative Ethics in Practice,* both available from Left Coast.

Chapter 5: Finding the Right Book Publisher

1. Another slick marketing idea of Amazon in order to sell Kindle readers and force you to buy all your eBooks from them. EBooks are no cheaper to produce than printed books, no matter what Amazon tells you.

2. In 2015, several college bookstores established arrangements with Amazon to service their textbook demand (Etherington 2015).

Chapter 6: The Book Proposal

1. Located at schooldata.com/wordpress/wp-content/uploads/2014/06/MDR-College-Catalog.pdf

Chapter 7: Writing the Damn Thing

1. I am not a qualitative researcher but an archaeologist. For my dissertation, I developed the concept of a "contested periphery" out of Immanuel Wallerstein's world-systems theory, where a marginal economic area is fought over by two superpowers. The diss was mediocre at best and never published. But enough people read it, picked up that term and have used it since then that I've become the Contested Periphery guy in archaeology, whatever that means.

References

Adler, Patricia A., Peter Adler, and John M. Johnson. 1992. Street Corner Society Revisited. Thematic issue of *Journal of Contemporary Ethnography* 21: 1.

Allen, Mitchell, 1992a. "Seeking a Publisher: Field Methods for Getting Published." *Cultural Anthropology Methods Newsletter* 4: 4–5.

Allen, Mitchell, 1992 b. "Hook, Line and Emptor: Preparing a Book Prospectus." *Cultural Anthropology Methods Newsletter* 4: 10–11.

Allen, Mitchell, 2014. "Networking Your Journal Article to Publication." International Institute for Qualitative Methodology blog. November 17. iiqm.wordpress.com/

Allen, Mitchell, 2015. "The Brave New World of Electronic Qualitative Publishing." *International Institute for Qualitative Inquiry Newsletter* 11.

Bowker, 2014. "Traditional Print Book Production Dipped Slightly in 2014." August 5. www.bowker.com/news/2014/Traditional-Print-Book-Production-Dipped-Slightly-in-2013.html, accessed June 3, 2015.

Economist, "Of Goats and Headaches." 2011. May 26. www.economist.com/node/18744177, accessed September 3, 2012.

Ellis, Carolyn. 1995. "Emotional and Ethical Quagmires of Returning to the Field." *Journal of Contemporary Ethnography* 24: 68–98.

Ellis, Carolyn. 2009. *Revision: Autoethnographic Reflections on Life and Work.* Walnut Creek, CA: Left Coast.

Etherington, Darrell, 2015. Amazon's First Staffed College Campus Store Should Have Retailers Worried. techcrunch.com/2015/02/03/amazon-campus-store/, accessed June 16, 2015.

Fagan, Brian. 2010. *Writing Archaeology: Telling Stories about the Past,* 2nd ed. Walnut Creek, CA: Left Coast.

Feather, John. 2007b. "Copyright and Literary Property" in Simon Eliot and Jonathan Rose, *A Companion to the History of the Book,* 520–530. Oxford: Blackwell.

Feather, John. 2007a. "The British Book Market 1600–1800" in Simon Eliot and Jonathan Rose, *A Companion to the History of the Book,* 232–246. Oxford: Blackwell.

Finkelstein, David, and Alistair McCleery. 2005. *An Introduction to Book History.* New York: Routledge.

Goodall, H. L., Jr. 2000. *Writing the New Ethnography.* Walnut Creek, CA: AltaMira.

Goodall, H. L., Jr. 2006. *A Need to Know: The Clandestine History of a CIA Family.* Walnut Creek, CA: Left Coast.

Goodall, H. L., Jr. 2008. *Writing Qualitative Inquiry.* Walnut Creek, CA: Left Coast.

Hellinga, Lotte. 2007. "The Gutenberg Revolutions" in Simon Eliot and Jonathan Rose, *A Companion to the History of the Book,* 207–219. Oxford: Blackwell.

Mayan, Maria J. 2012. "Spirited and Gutsy: Our Role as Qualitative Researchers." Keynote address at the 12th annual Thinking Qualitatively workshops. Edmonton, Alberta. June 18.

Milliot, Jim. 2014. "Industry Sales Flat in 2013; Trade Dropped 2.3%." *Publisher's Weekly,* June 26. www.publishersweekly.com/pw/by-topic/industry-news/financial-reporting/article/63052-industry-sales-flat-in-2013-trade-dropped-2-3.html

Milliot, Jim. 2015. "Amazon Lost $241 Million on $88 Billion in Sales." *Publisher's Weekly,* January 29. www.publishersweekly.com/pw/by-topic/industry-news/financial-reporting/article/65439-amazon-lost-241-million-on-88-billion-in-sales.html, accessed June 3, 2015.

Morse, Janice M. 2014. "Why We Blind: Anonymity in the Review Process." *Qualitative Health Research* 24: 1467–1468.

Morse, Janice M., and Jack Coulehan. 2015. "Maintaining Confidentiality in Qualitative Publications," *Qualitative Health Research* 25: 151–152.

Oxford University Press, *Annual Report of the Delegates of the University Press, 2010–2011*. fds.oup.com/www.oup.com/pdf/OUP_Annual_ Report_2010-11.pdf

Pelias, Ronald J. 2011. "Writing into Position: Strategies for Composition and Evaluation." In Norman K. Denzin and Yvonna S. Lincoln, *Handbook of Qualitative Research*, 4th ed., 659–668. Thousand Oaks, CA: Sage.

Powell, Walter. 1985. *Getting into Print: The Decision-Making Process in Scholarly Publishing*. Chicago: University of Chicago Press.

Poynter, Dan. 2015. Dan Poynter's Parapublishing.com. Statistics. bookstatistics.com/sites/para/resources/statistics.cfm, accessed June 15, 2015.

Richardson, Laurel, and Elizabeth Adams St. Pierre, "Writing: A Method of Inquiry." In Norman K. Denzin and Yvonna S. Lincoln, *Handbook of Qualitative Research*, 3rd ed., 959–978. Thousand Oaks CA: Sage.

Schmandt-Besserat, Denise. 1996. *How Writing Came About*. Austin: University of Texas Press.

Scholarly Open Access Nework, 2013. "The 'Open Research Network' Launches with 86 New OA Journals." May 28. scholarlyoa. com/2013/05/28/open-research-network/, accessed June 4, 2015.

Tolich, Martin, ed. 2015. *Qualitative Ethics in Practice*. Walnut Creek, CA: Left Coast.

Van den Hoonaard, Will, and Deborah K. van den Hoonaard. 2013. *Essentials of Thinking Ethically in Qualitative Research*. Walnut Creek, CA: Left Coast.

Ware, Mark, and Michael Mabe. 2012. *The STM Report: An Overview of Scientific and Scholarly Journals*, 3rd ed. The Hague: International Association of Scientific, Technical and Medical Publishers. www.stm-assoc.org/2012_12_11_STM_Report_2012.pdf

Wolcott, Harry F. 2009. *Writing Up Qualitative Research*, 3rd ed. Thousand Oaks, CA: Sage.

"The World's 56 Largest Book Publishers, 2014." 2014. *Publisher's Weekly*, June 27. www.publishersweekly.com/pw/by-topic/industry-news/ financial-reporting/article/63004-the-world-s-56-largest-book-publishers-2014.html, accessed June 3, 2015.

Index

About the Author

Mitchell Allen is Publisher of Left Coast Press, Inc., an academic press that specializes in publishing qualitative research methods and studies, including this book. A veteran of 40 years in publishing, his prior positions included Executive Editor at Sage Publications—where he created their qualitative research list—and Publisher of AltaMira Press. He was responsible for developing the *Handbook of Qualitative Research*, several leading qualitative journals, and dozens of other well-known qualitative publications. He is coauthor of *Getting Your Book Published* (Sage) and two dozen articles on publishing. Allen offers regular workshops on qualitative writing and publishing. He was given lifetime achievement awards from the International Congress of Qualitative Inquiry and the Society for the Study of Symbolic Interaction. Mitchell has a PhD from UCLA and teaches in the Sociology/Anthropology Department of Mills College in Oakland, California.

green press
INITIATIVE

Left Coast Press, Inc. is committed to preserving ancient forests and natural resources. We elected to print this title on 30% post consumer recycled paper, processed chlorine free. As a result, for this printing, we have saved:

2 Trees (40' tall and 6-8" diameter)
1 Million BTUs of Total Energy
128 Pounds of Greenhouse Gases
697 Gallons of Wastewater
47 Pounds of Solid Waste

Left Coast Press, Inc. made this paper choice because our printer, Thomson-Shore, Inc., is a member of Green Press Initiative, a nonprofit program dedicated to supporting authors, publishers, and suppliers in their efforts to reduce their use of fiber obtained from endangered forests.

For more information, visit www.greenpressinitiative.org

Environmental impact estimates were made using the Environmental Defense Paper Calculator. For more information visit: www.papercalculator.org.